Manijeh

Not Only a Change of Name

Manijeh

Not Only a Change of Name

Manijeh Saatchi
with the assistance of Fereshteh Hooshmand

George Ronald, Publisher
Oxford

George Ronald, Publisher
Oxford
www.grbooks.com

First published in Australia in 2010

Reprinted 2014, 2021

ISBN 978-0-85398-572-3

A catalogue record for this book is available
from the British Library

Cover photography by Sahba Roshan

Original book design by Armon Rostami, modified
for this GR edition

Cover design Rene Steiner, Steinergraphics.com

Contents

Foreword, *by Peter Khan* vii

Acknowledgements ix

1 Childhood 1

2 Javad and His Family 8

3 Bushehr 32

4 Pilgrims 47

5 The Destruction of the House of the Báb 56

6 Fere and Abbas 62

7 Revolution and Persecution 69

8 After Javad 79

9 Visitors from Australia 94

10 Getting Out 103

11 Faranak's Story 125

12 Going Home 136

Epilogue, *by Fereshteh Hooshmand* 153

Foreword

This book is a testimony to the resilience of the human spirit. It describes the indomitable courage and determination of a woman who sought to find and follow religious truth despite the implacable opposition of her family and friends.

Manijeh, whose life is chronicled in this book, emerges as an individual of deeply-rooted conviction, unswerving in her adherence to principle, and consistent in her action despite relentless persecution, criticism and harassment from those who might reasonably have been expected to display compassion and fair-mindedness. It is a measure of the strength of her belief that she refused to compromise its foundational precepts in the face of the pressures exerted on her by civil and ecclesiastical authorities.

Vividly portrayed here is the deplorable condition into which Iranian society has now sunk, as a direct consequence of several decades of rule by fanatical and narrow-minded clerics. The rule of law has been subverted, the exercise of rational thought has been discredited, and rank ignorance is given free rein. The mass of the people remain intellectually fettered, deprived of the freedom to question the ideological constraints imposed on them or to engage in their own independent investigation of truth.

One cannot but be distressed that a country of such talent and endowment, which has been in centuries past a world-renowned centre of culture and enlightenment, has been reduced to its present condition. Its many admirers must await patiently for the dark clouds now enshrouding it to be dissipated, and for its pristine radiance to be restored.

This book describes a degree of hardship to which very few people are subjected in the course of their lives. Manijeh's beloved husband's untimely death occurs as a consequence of an assault instigated by those opposed to his religious beliefs. Her children are exposed to constant humiliation and discrimination, their education interrupted or terminated. Family assets are confiscated by unscrupulous officials, with no legal justification or redress. Members of her family are reduced to poverty through the operation of schemes designed to deprive them of professional opportunities and income.

However, this is not a book of lamentation; far from it. It is a record of the power of the human spirit to withstand even the most perfidious oppressors and to emerge triumphant from persecution. As such it conveys a message of hope and optimism for all who value truth and who yearn for justice to prevail.

Peter Khan

Acknowledgements

This is a story of love, belief and triumph that began through the eyes of an unassuming young girl and ends with me as a grandmother, matured by years, mellowed by life's hardships and reborn through faith. This is the story of the girl I was, the young woman I would become and the grandmother I am today. Like the countless untold stories of my generation, this story is a reflection of my inner being. My part in the history I will recount for you is minor. This book could never hope to be a comprehensive account of the events that took place during this momentous chapter in the history of my homeland. Only a handful of the many individuals and families who shaped my life and my experience find mention, yet their place in my heart and memory remains sacred and vivid.

Despite the tragic and sometimes harrowing events I recount here, my love for and devotion to the country of my birth and the cradle of my Faith remain strong and unswerving. My memories are forever entwined with its glorious history, which holds in its far reaches the echoes of my laughter and tears. I long for the day when Iran will shimmer with its former glory and shine resplendent among its peers.

I am totally appreciative of and indebted to my daughter Fere for the enormous time and effort she put into writing my story. Without her dedication and commitment to this project, it would not have been possible to publish this book. I wish to thank Rhian Williams, Sandy Riching and Jackie Courtney for their sincere efforts in reading and reviewing the first and second draft. My deepest gratitude also goes to Michael Day for initial editing of the manuscript. My gratitude must also go to my son-in-law Abbas, who welcomed me into his home and patiently supported his wife as we spent many late nights recording this story. I wish to especially thank my grandsons for their support and their continued encouragement. I acknowledge the role of many friends and relatives for their love and devotion.

My special gratitude goes to the Bahá'í World Centre and the National Spiritual Assembly of the Bahá'ís of Australia and their dedicated staff for their research to ensure the accuracy of the historical information contained here. Last but not least, I would like to extend my gratitude to the Arts Council of Australia for its support of this project through its Multicultural Grants Scheme.

Manijeh Saatchi

1

Childhood

My name is Manijeh now. When I was born on 29 August 1929 in a city called Jahrom in Fars in a country now called Iran, I was given the name of Fatimih. I was born into a Shi'ite Muslim family, the oldest of five children, three boys and another girl. My family were not wealthy, and most of my early years were spent on our family farm on the outskirts of Shiraz. My family struggled, as did most of our friends, to make ends meet in an increasingly difficult market. We contended with poverty, illness, and poor harvests year after year.

I was seven years old when after a particularly poor harvest we moved from our farm to the bustling city of Shiraz. What little we owned we packed into bundles and took with us, and soon found board with a woman named Nahid, whose husband had died not long before. We rented a small room in Nahid's house, and our presence there helped her pay the bills and support her young son Nasser.

The house we shared with Nahid was in a suburb of Shiraz near the famous mosque called Shah-i-Chiraq. The neighbourhood children used to play outside the mosque and I would continually marvel at the array of people that came and went from its doors. The mosque was ornately decorated with mosaic tiles and had beautiful, glittering glass chandeliers. Its portals were crowned with 40-metre-tall minarets. A golden dome dominated the mosque itself. Before entering, visitors would take their shoes off and never be guaranteed the shoes would be there upon their return. The sight of this steady stream of pilgrims was a constant source of interest to me. The women who entered the mosque always wore the *chador* (the long black cape worn by Iranian women), which was used to cover their bodies from head to toe, only showing their faces. This shapeless garb was seen as a means by which women could retain their modesty and purity and not become the object of men's desires.

As a girl growing up in Iran, I began wearing a *hejab*, a scarf covering the head and shoulders, when I was eight. It was from this age onwards that young girls in Iran were groomed for the role of wife and mother, and despite my pleas to be allowed to go to school, my mother refused on the grounds that girls who went to school ended up as prostitutes. Though I soon came to see this for the poor excuse it was, there was little merit in arguing with my mother and I reluctantly stayed at home. I soon became occupied with the household chores which, my mother assured me, would be good training for when I married.

Throughout this period, I was increasingly envious of the boys around me who would go to school each day and were also given other luxuries such as running errands, going shopping and even, in some cases, working after school. I often dreamed of how different my life would be if I were a boy. This fantasy sustained me as I watched my brothers and other children enjoy a freedom I was denied.

Among the boys who went to school each day was the son of our landlady. Nasser was an only child and a gentle boy. He was tall and handsome and had big brown eyes that seemed to dominate his entire face. He was quiet and shy with those around him, yet his care and attention was always influenced by his sense of justice and compassion. I don't know whether he really was such an exceptionally good boy or whether it merely seemed that way because I liked him. When other children would bully me, Nasser would always jump to my defence. When squabbles broke out among the neighbourhood children, Nasser always took it upon himself to find an outcome that would make everyone happy. One of the qualities I admired most in Nasser was his sense of equality. He would often tell the other children that the only difference between boys and girls was their outward appearance but that in all other ways they should be treated equally. For a boy of his age growing up in Iran, these were radical ideas which set him apart from his peers, who still believed a girl's place was at home. Nasser was a peacemaker in every sense of the word, and he would always defend our 'peace' in whatever way he could. This simple philosophy became significant for me, even as a child; I knew that when Nasser was around I would feel peace.

Despite his peace-loving nature, the neighbourhood children could often be heard calling him '*kafar*', which meant infidel. The children would not include him in any game which included physical contact, as they would say that he was '*najess*' or unclean. It would break my heart to see other children ridicule him in this way, especially when he always treated everyone with such fairness and respect. I later discovered that Nasser and his mother were Bahá'ís and that was why the other children would call him an infidel and say that he was unclean. I found this idea of belittling someone for what they believed confusing, much more so when I saw the way which Nahid and Nasser treated all those around them.

One night, not long after we moved in with Nahid and Nasser, I overheard my mother saying to my father, 'A Báhá'í will have her over my dead body!' This frightened me and I thought that maybe someone was going to kill me. When I tried to ask my mother what she had meant, I was scolded and told to mind my own business. I discovered a few days later that Nahid had encouraged my mother to send me to school. I heard my mother complaining to my father, 'What does Nahid want? It is none of her business.' My father answered, 'She has a son. What do you expect? Maybe she wants an educated wife for him.'

My parents asked me if Nahid had talked to me about going to school. I was worried about telling the truth because I could see that they were already displeased with something Nahid had said or done, but I was also worried about lying to them. I replied truthfully that Nahid had told me that the education of girls was more important than boys because if girls went to school then they could educate their own children.

This incensed my mother, who told my father that

Nahid had said much the same thing to her. I was to learn later that Nahid had not only encouraged my mother to send me to school but had also said that Nasser liked me quite a bit and had proposed that we marry when I was older. I wonder now whether my mother was more concerned at the thought of her daughter being educated or at the idea of her marrying an infidel. My mother was convinced that any education for me would be detrimental and that I would become a 'bad' girl. Despite Nahid's encouragement, my mother flatly refused to entertain any idea of sending me to school, and that matter was never discussed again.

My mother soon came to realize the influence that Nahid was having over me and how I delighted both in her company and Nasser's. My mother became inherently suspicious of Nahid and would spy on her at any opportunity. When Nahid and Nasser left the house at night to attend Bahá'í meetings, my mother concluded that whatever they did at these meeting was at best immoral. She tried to convince me that Nahid and her son were infidels and should be shunned at every turn.

The more condemnatory my mother was of Nahid and Nasser and their beliefs, the more interested I became in who these Bahá'ís were. I couldn't accept that this mother and son whom I had grown to love and respect and who always treated everyone with the utmost kindness and love could be half the things my mother accused them of being. Among the many things that Nahid taught me was that I should love everyone, whether they were Christians, Jews, Muslims or Bahá'ís. When my mother heard me repeating this, she scolded me and said, 'Stop that nonsense! Don't you repeat that or I will lock you up for weeks and feed you on bread and water.' So shocked was I by her threat that I thought I would never dare to speak my mind again. My mother told me again that they were all '*najess*' and that she didn't know anything about the spiritual kingdom, but all she knew was that there were lots of prophets before Muhammad but none after. As a young child, I had little choice but to agree with my mother and agree with her ideas, whether they made sense to me or not. I quietly acquiesced and refrained from talking about the conversations that Nahid and I had, yet in my heart of hearts I felt sure that my parents were the most intolerant people on earth.

My mother had few solutions to my new-found interest in Nahid's ideas of the world. She would threaten me with the fire of hell, to which I would respond that Nahid had told me that God loves everybody. In desperation one Friday, my mother forced me to go with her to the Friday prayers at the mosque. It was Ramadan (the Islamic month of fasting), and the streets of Shiraz were buzzing with people. In that particular year, Ramadan had fallen right in the middle of a very hot summer and the clergy were serving ice cream in the mosques for people to break their fast. My mother said we could sit in the front when they served the ice cream and then move to the back row for a second serving. My mother talked to the mullah at length that evening, and I couldn't help but wonder whether my new-found ideas and Nahid's influence were the subject of their discussion.

We hurried home after the prayers in the mosque were finished. I soon discovered that in her conversation with the mullah, my mother had reached a decision which would forever change the course of my life. When we arrived home, my mother announced that we would be moving house. She ordered us to pack our belongings that very night. I was devastated and began to cry. My mother scolded me and ordered me to start packing. In the middle of the night we took all our belongings one by one and walked to another house that my mother had secured on a temporary basis. I thought often of making some noise to wake Nahid up, but the fear of my mother prevented me. Broken-hearted, I watched as my family left a home I had come to love. Most painful of all was that I didn't have a chance to say goodbye to Nahid and Nasser. As we left their house and walked to our new home, two things were certain for me – I knew that I would become a Bahá'í and I secretly hoped that I would grow up and one day marry Nasser.

2

Javad and His Family

It was the middle of the night when we arrived at the house of a woman whose husband had died several years earlier in Iraq. This family were Muslim Sufis, and I am sure my mother felt that I would be safe from the influence of infidels in a good Muslim home.

The experience of leaving Nahid's home had been emotionally and physically exhausting. We worked throughout the night to move our belongings, and it was only when morning broke that we finally completed the task. By sunrise I was exhausted, but curious enough to want to learn more about this new family we had come to live with.

As our two families sat in the front yard becoming better acquainted, my mother began to criticize Nahid, accusing her of trying to 'steal' me. The conversation continued with my mother painting the worst possible picture of this loving family. When she began to describe them as 'infidels' and 'untouchables', I excused myself and went into the house. I missed everything about Nahid and Nasser – their home, their love and compassion, their gentleness and care. In the short time in Nasser's house, I had learned more about myself than ever before and had become even more convinced that my mother's ideas were nothing more than narrow-minded bigotry.

As the days and weeks progressed, we began to learn

more about our new hosts. Their son Javad, who spoke both Arabic and Persian (Farsi), particularly intrigued me. I had never known anyone who could speak two languages. We learned over time that Javad's father had been Haji Ali Aqa Shirazi, known amongst his thousands of followers as the prominent Shamshir Ali Shah, a famous Sufi. Between 1912 and 1914, just before the First World War, Shamshir Ali Shah, his family and some of his followers had travelled to Karbila. Once the war broke out they were forced to stay in Karbila and could not return to Iran. After it ended, Shamshir Ali Shah went to Mecca on pilgrimage. There he told his followers that he would journey on to the holy city of Medina, asking them to return to Khoramshahr (a city in the south of Iran) and await his return. During his absence, it was rumoured that instead of travelling to Medina, Shamshir Ali Shah had travelled to Akka in Palestine, where Bahá'u'lláh, the Prophet-Founder of the Bahá'í Faith, had been exiled as a prisoner in the nineteenth century.

When Shamshir Ali Shah returned, he was poisoned by one of his followers, who feared that the Sufi cleric had found truth in the teachings of this exiled prisoner. Almost immediately after his death Shamshir Ali Shah's followers became bewildered and disunited. Some looked to his young sons for leadership, others rushed into his house and took whatever they considered to be a blessed item as a token of remembrance. The end of this turmoil left the family in a state of poverty, and eventually Javad, his mother and three siblings fled to Shiraz.

My mother and Javad's mother would often sit in the

front yard and, as they went on with the chores of the day and the preparation of food, would have long conversations about their children and what was best for them. It was during one of these conversations that I learned that Javad's mother was actually his maternal aunt and that his real mother had died when he was very young. I felt sorry for Javad and thought that he must also know what it was like to be alone. Despite working and trying to support his aunt and other siblings, Javad always had time for the rest of the children, and he would entertain us in the evening by reading the poems of Hafiz. He would ask each one of us in turn to close our eyes and make a wish, and then he would close his eyes and open the book and whichever poem appeared would somehow seem to answer our wishes. On one occasion when it was my turn, I quietly wished to go to Nahid's house for a visit. He turned to me with a look that seemed to understand, and recited the following poem by heart:

LOOKING FOR YOUR FACE

From the beginning of my life
I have been looking for your face
but today I have seen it.

Today I have seen
the charm, the beauty,
the unfathomable grace
of the face
that I was looking for.

Today I have found you
and those that laughed
and scorned me yesterday
are sorry that they were not looking
as I did.

I am bewildered by the magnificence
of your beauty
and wish to see you with a hundred eyes.

My heart has burned with passion
and has searched forever
for this wondrous beauty
that I now behold.

I am ashamed
to call this love human
and afraid of God
to call it divine.

Your fragrant breath
like the morning breeze
has come to the stillness of the garden
You have breathed new life into me
I have become your sunshine
and also your shadow.

My soul is screaming in ecstasy
Every fibre of my being
is in love with you.

Your effulgence
has lit a fire in my heart
and you have made radiant
for me
the earth and sky.

My arrow of love
has arrived at the target
I am in the house of mercy
and my heart
is a place of prayer.

I didn't fully understand what he meant, but I felt he could read my mind. My mother loved the poem and said it was from the *Gulistan* of Sa'di, but Javad said it was from Rumi. My father told Javad that he was a very humble man. He said to my mother that if she liked poems by Sa'di, he knew one by heart. Then he started reciting the following poem:

From my beloved's hand there came one day,
whilst in the garden a piece of scented clay –
'And art thou musk or attar? Say from whence
Comes that sweet odour that o'erpowers my sense?'
'Nay, I'm a worthless thing' – the clay replied –
'But having waited by the rose's side,
My soul absorbed my sweet companion's worth,
Else I'd remain, as rest, – a clod of earth!'

I didn't understand that one either but everyone seemed to be pleased.

More often than not my mother would complain to Javad's aunt that I was becoming an impossible child. 'I don't understand her any more,' my mother would lament. 'If it is sunny, she prays for rain. If it is wet, she prays for sun. Every breath follows the last, praying to God for something. Why can't she go and play in the lane like other children any more?' Javad's aunt considered this for a moment before turning to my mother and saying, 'She is becoming a woman.' I overheard this exchange and was most impressed that Javad's aunt would consider me so mature to call me a 'woman'. Even though I was only nine years old and clearly just a young girl, I hoped that with this description of womanhood I might gain a little more respect and understanding.

The days passed, and my mother and Javad's aunt would temper the mundane tasks of the household with endless gossip about the children. They would make decisions for us as though we didn't exist. The fate of the girls was always much worse. We belonged first to our fathers and then to our husbands. Our opinion simply didn't matter, nor was it ever either asked for or heard. If my mother wasn't lamenting the burden of her life, she was condemning other people for theirs. Nahid and her ideas and influence over me were regular topics of conversation, and my mother took great delight in explaining to Javad's aunt that the local mullah agreed with everything she said. According to my mother, the mullah had said that the Bahá'í Faith was not a true religion and was at odds with Islam and its central belief that Muhammad was the last of God's prophets.

I knew better than to argue with my mother, but as I overheard these conversations, I became more and more certain that both the mullah and my mother were wrong. As a Muslim child I had been raised to believe in a God Who was compassionate and all-powerful. It simply didn't make sense that a kind and compassionate God would stop sending prophets to show us the way. Just as God had sent Moses and Jesus and Muhammad, surely it was possible that he had also sent Bahá'u'lláh. I felt alone in my thinking and certain that I would never find any support for my ideas among the families I knew. It was therefore a pleasant surprise for me when Javad and I became better acquainted and I learned that he too was much more open-minded than his aunt or my mother.

It took several months before Javad and I became friends. It was most uncommon for boys and girls to mingle with each other outside the bounds of their own family. Living in the same house as Javad and his family, it was a little easier and, in time, we felt comfortable talking with one another. When I got to know him a little better, I told Javad about Nahid and Nasser and how my mother had forced us to leave in the middle of the night, and how I had grown to love this mother and son with whom I had no right to associate because of their Faith. Javad was clearly touched by my plight. He told me that his boss at the textile factory was a Bahá'í and that the majority of his employees were Bahá'ís too. Javad told me that he had always known the Bahá'ís to be kind and trustworthy people and that surely that was most important. Javad explained that he thought in some way it was his calling to find out more about the Bahá'ís and what they believed. His father, Shamshir Ali Shah, had met a dervish in the mountains of Kurdistan who had told him that two of his children would find the truth for themselves and Shamshir Ali Shah had told Javad that he was one of those children.

I was relieved and grateful that Javad shared the same sense of acceptance of the Bahá'ís as I did. He was following a legacy his father had left him before his passing and I was following the example of Nahid and Nasser whom I had come to love and respect. In a country where the Bahá'ís were being persecuted, they had found unlikely support from two children.

I was to learn later that among the advice that the mullah had seen fit to give to my mother was his suggestion that I marry as soon as possible. The mullah felt that marriage would surely tame my inquisitiveness and, if I married, I would become consumed with the care of a husband and household and would have little time to speculate about other things. My mother took this advice seriously and several months later she announced that the mullah would soon come to read a verse for Javad and me. This verse would make Javad and me '*halal*', a Muslim term meaning lawful. She said that a man and a woman could not live in the same house, under the same roof, if they were not *halal*. She also said Javad could be my guardian after my father died. I was oblivious to what was happening and thought that becoming *halal* would make Javad and me like brother and sister. In order to ensure that I cooperated with her plan, my mother promised to buy me a red dress that I had seen in the bazaar on the way to Friday prayers. She promised that I could wear the red dress when the mullah came, but only if I was a good girl and listened to what she said. It seemed a reasonable deal to me. Javad and I would become brother and sister, I would get the red dress, and my mother would be happy.

On the day the mullah arrived, I was busy playing outside with other children. My mother called me to come inside, but I was too occupied with a game of hide and seek to worry about my mother's business. At first I even refused to change my clothes or brush my hair. There were lots of stern-looking adults in the room and I felt both shy and scared. I wondered why they were there. My mother became incensed at my lack of cooperation. She said that if I didn't behave myself, she would cut my hair short, wouldn't let me wear my red dress, wouldn't allow me to play in the lane again and wouldn't feed me for a week until I died. I loved my red dress and I certainly didn't want to die. I felt I had no choice but to give in and do what she wanted me to do. When my mother finally dragged me inside I saw my father receiving money from a man I didn't know. I thought it an odd time to conduct a business transaction. I later learned that Javad's uncle had paid my father a dowry on Javad's behalf. After changing my clothes, my mother took me to a room full of women who were covered from head to toe in their *chadors*. She ordered me to sit down next to her on the floor, as was the custom. No one said anything about my red dress.

Just before the mullah came in, they covered my head

with a cloth and although I couldn't see, I was aware that the mullah sat opposite my mother and me. I didn't understand the Arabic verses he recited but suddenly my mother told me to say 'Yes'. I asked why. She kept pinching me on both of my legs insisting that I say 'Yes' to the mullah. Eventually I got fed up and said 'Yes' to see what would happen. The other women cheered happily and said, 'There's a good girl.' I was glad that I had done the right thing and that everyone was so pleased.

Everyone stayed and enjoyed themselves and I was glad that I had behaved myself at the event. Only later in the evening, when I overhead Javad's aunt tell my mother that 'something was meant to happen', did I become confused. My mother told me not to scream, shout or cry and this confused me even more. I thought someone was going to kill me and became terrified of what was going to happen. Later, when Javad and I were left alone together in the bedroom, it suddenly occurred to me that maybe we had been married. Javad seemed happy. I trusted that he would be able to help me understand what had happened. Javad thought that all boys and girls were like us and that this marriage ritual was just a normal and natural part of growing up. He didn't seem to think that it mattered that I was only nine and he was 16. And in the time and culture we were living in, it really didn't matter.

I wasn't at all comfortable being alone with Javad. We were both self-conscious and I felt sold and cheated by my own parents. Javad sensed my distress and suggested that if I wasn't ready we could wait to consummate our marriage. I was relieved and grateful that he was kind-hearted enough to at least allow me to decide when I was ready to have a sexual relationship. While this eased my concern, it didn't solve the other problem that both Javad and I knew we had to face. My mother and Javad's aunt would be expecting the marriage to be consummated and, as was customary, would be waiting to see proof that I had been a virgin. Traditionally the bride and groom would produce a handkerchief or the bed sheets, and the trace of blood would prove the bride's virginity and that the marriage had been consummated. Javad suggested that we pierce the tips of our fingers and smear the blood on a handkerchief and pretend that we had consummated our marriage. We took a secret vow that we would have a real physical relationship when I was ready and perhaps much older than my nine years.

Despite our attempts, our families were not convinced; we would often be left alone together and then interrogated about whether we had in fact consummated our marriage or not. At last the pressure became too much, so out of a sense of duty and in order to stop the constant harassment by my mother and Javad's aunt, we finally consummated our marriage in a brief and all too unpleasant episode. The experience for me was as humiliating as I could have ever imagined, and although Javad was both patient and considerate, I was devastated by being forced to do something I was not ready for. Javad saw my great distress and we agreed that our relationship would remain platonic until I was older and ready to decide for myself. And all the while my thoughts were on one thing – I wanted to be with Nasser.

As our married life began, Javad did his very best to make me happy. He continued to work at the textile factory and I busied myself with the chores my mother would set. Married life didn't seem to afford me much in the way of privilege, except that now Javad was responsible for me, and I had the freedom on some occasions to accompany him outside the house. One such outing was to the home of Javad's employer where a learned man was going to speak about the prophecies of the Qur'án. Javad had asked if the talk would have anything to do with the Bahá'í Faith and whether he could bring me. Javad had promised to take me to meet Bahá'ís if he could and he was happy that on this occasion he could fulfil his promise. He believed that if we searched for the truth together, we would also grow closer and be happy.

Javad and I were welcomed into the home of his employer, Mr Dehghan, and we soon saw that there were many people there who had come to hear the learned man speak. The gathering began with a round of prayers. Some people said prayers that they had memorized, others read from a book. I did neither because I couldn't read, and I knew no prayers by heart except the obligatory prayer. Javad said a prayer for his parents, but I found it difficult to pray for my parents. I didn't understand everything that was said that night but I enjoyed the talk of the learned speaker and the company of the Bahá'ís who were there. The speaker, Mr Chehrenegar, invited us to visit him whenever we wanted. Both Javad and I looked forward to the visits we would have with them.

On most occasions, my parents and Javad's aunt didn't

ask where we were going, and we didn't tell them. Both Javad and I knew that if we wanted to enjoy this freedom and associate with our Bahá'í friends, we would have to keep our visits a secret from our families. For us, our association with the Bahá'ís was a passionate statement of independence. I had reclaimed my right to visit a Bahá'í house and Javad had started fulfilling his dream of searching for the truth. Perhaps we would have done this without each other, but it would have been such a struggle for me and I know that I would have been extremely lonely. If I had known marrying Javad would have brought such freedom, I would have readily and gladly said 'Yes'.

One of the most refreshing aspects of our visit to the home of the Bahá'ís was that we were always welcomed and made to feel at home. Unlike in other households where girls were only allowed to associate with visitors if the latter were proposing marriage, and even then their role was to serve tea and quietly sit in the background, at the home of the Bahá'ís we were welcomed and invited to join in the conversations and discussion. On one particular occasion, I remember one of the Bahá'ís explaining that men and women were like the two wings of a bird. If the bird had two strong wings, then the bird could fly evenly in the sky. If one wing was weak, the bird couldn't fly and would suffer. It was an analogy that Javad and I enjoyed and remembered.

For Javad in particular, the sense of community that he felt among the Bahá'ís, and their welcoming acceptance of people from all beliefs and backgrounds, gave him a great sense of belonging. As a Muslim Sufi from

Iraq growing up in Iran, Javad had suffered taunts and insults because he was not Persian. Although he was a friend to everyone, his friendship was often not repaid. At times the prejudice he suffered became intolerable. The Bahá'ís we knew created an environment where we could be ourselves. We had a free choice to participate, listen, learn, share our opinions and enjoy the friendship of many different people.

The years passed. Both Javad and I grew up and matured, which was a credit more to our own sense of discovery than anything we learned from my parents or Javad's family. I was nearly 13 years old when Javad went to Bushehr, a small town 300 kilometres from Shiraz, to visit his sister. Two months passed and there was no sign of his return. I felt very lonely. I took inspiration and courage from a wonderful summer's day and decided that it was time for me to visit Nahid and Nasser. I wanted to see Nasser and tell him what had happened to me in the years since we left their home. I found my way there and gently knocked on the door. Nahid opened it and greeted me with open arms – for me, it was like coming home. Nahid asked about our lives and what had happened after we left that night with no warning. I told her that I had missed them and that was all I wanted to say. Nahid looked at me in a way that made me feel that she noticed my eyebrows had been plucked. Traditionally this was done only to girls who were married and so Nahid asked me if I was married. Despite my admiration and respect for Javad, I regretted having to say that I was. Nahid congratulated me and asked about my husband.

I told her about Javad and explained that maybe it was not my destiny to marry Nasser, but both Javad and I had many Bahá'í friends and we were learning as much as we could about the Bahá'í Faith. Nahid was genuinely happy for me and assured me that Nasser would be too. She told me that Nasser was busy with his studies and had not married yet. I left Nahid's house feeling at least that I had had the chance to say goodbye.

When Javad returned from his trip to Bushehr, we were invited to a celebration marking the anniversary of the Birth of Bahá'u'lláh on 12 November. This coincided with the first day of the Muslim month of Muharram, which is a significant month of mourning for Muslims, during which they wear black. When we arrived at the home of these Bahá'ís, the lady of the house offered me a green dress and said that it was an evening of celebration. Since they had not been present at our wedding, our hosts gave us gifts and showed us immense generosity and kindness. I felt that it was the way my wedding should have been, and both Javad and I rejoiced and delighted in the company of these friends. Quite apart from their principles of unity and equality, what I found most attractive about the Bahá'ís was their unconditional love for Javad and me. I frequently thought that when I grew up I would be just as loving to others as the Bahá'ís had been to me. On that memorable night, our host talked about the significance of the Bahá'í Holy Days and touched on the history of the Bahá'í Faith. At the end of the evening and after much prayerful thought, Javad announced that he wished to become a Bahá'í and declared his belief in Bahá'u'lláh and the teachings of the Bahá'í Faith. I was so happy for him. The truth his father had searched for, Javad had now found. I too wished to declare myself to be a Bahá'í, but according to Bahá'í law one must wait to be 15 years old. I was content to bask in the happiness of Javad and our friends and know that I too had found the truth and that in my heart I was already a Bahá'í. I said a quiet prayer then for Nahid and Nasser, who had started me on my own search for truth. I somehow felt that they knew I would find it.

The joy and elation of that night stayed with me for years to come and through the many hardships that would follow. When we arrived home that evening, my excitement was too much to contain and, forgetting our promise not to say anything of our visit to the Bahá'ís, I announced to all that Javad and I were Bahá'ís. My mother looked at us with a horror that I had never seen, nor would ever see again. She called us 'God-forsaken infidels' and said we had blasphemed against God. She demanded that I divorce Javad or I would follow him into the fire of hell. As calmly as I could, I explained that it was she who had given me to Javad in the first place and that was her decision, but that now it was my own decision, I would never divorce Javad. I knew then that whatever the future would hold for us, we had the same dream and the same hopes for the future. We had found the truth together and together we were going to stay.

My mother accused us of selling our religion for 'a few lousy presents' and we were told to pack our belongings and leave the house before the others were contaminated by our blasphemous thoughts. Our two families started fighting, blaming each other for what they saw as the greatest of all tragedies. Javad's aunt said I had been mentally unstable from the beginning and my mother called them 'bloody Sufis'. Javad and I went to our rooms and started packing. We left our house just before dawn; soon afterwards we were on the streets of Shiraz, homeless and without food. We spent the day in the mosque and then as the sun set we went back to the home of our Bahá'í friends. We stayed there for some time while we sought their advice on what we should do. It was clear to both of us that we wanted to be part of making the world a better place and sharing the truth that we had found with others. We might have been dreamers, but we knew that if our dreams had brought us this far, they could take us further. I remembered the way Nasser had always wanted things to be peaceful. I promised then that I would work towards that dream for him as well as myself. I told Javad about the significant role Nahid and Nasser had played in cultivating my philosophy of life. They had planted the seed of faith in my heart, and now I was ready to seize my chance. We were both grateful for everything Nahid and Nasser had done for me.

Despite the generosity of our hosts, both Javad and I had a strong desire to leave Shiraz and begin life on our own, whatever challenges we were likely to face. One day, while deep in thought and prayer, I felt an unconscious voice telling me that Javad and I should travel to Bushehr. At first I thought this was likely to be a simple desire to see Javad's sister, but I felt sure that, whatever the reason,

Bushehr was where we should go. Javad agreed with me. We discussed our plans with our host. We explained that we wanted to share our ideas and thoughts with other people, just as the Bahá'ís in Shiraz had shared their ideas with us. Javad explained that we both wanted to be a catalyst for changing the society we lived in. Javad had read many things about the Bahá'í Faith and he was convinced that the principles the Faith offered were a clear remedy for the problems society faced. I explained that my ardent wish and desire was to be able to share these ideas with children, just as Nahid had shared these ideas with me. After much discussion and inquiries, we learned that not only was it possible for us to move to Bushehr, but that the Bahá'í community there would be happy to have our services as custodians of the House of the Báb in that city. With the help of our hosts and Bahá'í friend in Shiraz, we learned a great deal about the life of the Báb and his station as a Prophet of God in preparation for our journey to Bushehr and our role as caretakers of that House.

The early 19th century had been a period of great expectations in religious circles. Scientific inquiry, industrialization and progress led many earnest believers from all religious backgrounds to turn to the scriptures of their Faiths for an understanding of the accelerating processes of change. In Europe and America, groups like the Templers and the Millerites believed they had found in the Christian scriptures evidence supporting their belief that history had ended and the return of Jesus Christ was at hand. A similar thinking took hold among many groups of Muslims in the Middle East, who came to believe that the fulfilment of various prophecies in the Qur'án and the Islamic Traditions was imminent. One of the most dramatic of these movements emerged in Iran. It focused on the person and teachings of a young merchant from the city of Shiraz named Siyyid 'Alí-Muḥammad, known to history as the Báb. In 1844 in Shiraz, the Báb announced that the Day of God was at hand and that He was Himself the One promised in Islamic scripture. The Bábí Faith was founded on 23 May 1844 when the Báb announced that He was Islam's promised Qa'im.

History records that the Báb was an extraordinary child. Born on 20 October 1819, He possessed a surprising wisdom and nobility, reminiscent of the young Jesus. Upon reaching manhood, the Báb joined his uncle in the family business, a trading house, and divided his time between Shiraz and the port city of Bushehr. His integrity and piety won the esteem of the other merchants with whom He came in contact. The poor also knew him for His generosity. After His announcement that he was the promised Qa'im, the Báb attracted followers rapidly, and the new religious movement spread through Iran like wildfire. This growth stirred opposition and persecution, especially among the religious establishment, who saw in the new Faith a threat to their own power and prestige. In the course of this persecution, the Báb was imprisoned several times. His major work, the Bayán, abrogated certain Muslim laws and replaced them with new ones. It emphasized a high moral standard, with an emphasis on purity of heart and motive. It also upheld the station of women and the poor, and it promoted education and useful sciences. The central theme of the Bayán was the appearance of a second Messenger from God, one Who would be far greater than the Báb, and Whose mission would be to usher in the age of peace and plenty that had for so long been promised in Islam, as well as in Judaism, Christianity and all the other world religions.

In some respects (although not all), the Báb's role can be compared to that of John the Baptist in the founding of Christianity. The Báb was Bahá'u'lláh's Herald. His primary mission was to prepare the way for Bahá'u'lláh to reveal in 1863 that He was a Manifestation of God. At the same time, however, the Báb founded a distinctive and independent religion of his own. Although the young merchant's given name was Siyyid 'Alí-Muḥammad, He took the title 'Báb', meaning 'Gate' or 'Door' in Arabic. His coming, the Báb explained, represented the portal through which the universal Messenger of God expected by all humanity would soon appear.

By proclaiming an entirely new religion, the Báb was able to help His followers break free entirely from the Islamic frame of reference and to mobilize them in preparation for the coming of Bahá'u'lláh. The boldness of this proclamation stirred intense fear within the religious and secular establishments. Accordingly, persecution of the Bábís quickly developed. Those opposed to the Báb ultimately argued that He was not only a heretic, but also a dangerous rebel. The authorities decided to have Him executed.

On 9 July 1850, this sentence was carried out in the courtyard of the Tabriz army barracks. Some 10,000 people crowded the rooftops of the barracks and houses that overlooked the square. Two ropes against a wall suspended the Báb and a young follower. A regiment of 750 Armenian soldiers, arranged in three files of 250 each, opened fire in three successive volleys. So dense was the smoke raised by the gunpowder and dust that the sky was darkened and the entire yard obscured. As recorded in an account filed with the British Foreign Office, the Báb was not to be seen when the smoke cleared. His companion stood uninjured and untouched by the bullets. The ropes by which he and the Báb had been suspended were rent into pieces. The Báb was found back in His cell, giving final instructions to one of His followers. Earlier in the day, when the guards had come to take Him to the execution ground, the Báb had warned that no 'earthly power' could silence Him until He had finished all that He had to say. Now, when the guards arrived a second time, the Báb calmly announced: 'Now you may proceed to fulfil your intention.' For the second time, the Báb and His young companion were brought out for execution. The Armenian troops refused to fire again, and a Muslim firing squad was assembled and ordered to shoot. This time, the bodies of the pair were shattered, their bones and flesh mingled into one mass. Surprisingly, their faces were untouched. Thus ended the life of the Herald of the Bahá'í Faith, although the fire of the revelation He had revealed was to blaze on.

To have the honour of looking after the House of the Báb was beyond our comprehension. It was only in later years that we would truly understand the blessing and bounty we had been given. After days of preparation, we said goodbye to our Bahá'í friends in Shiraz and set off on what was to be a three-day journey to Bushehr. It was in 1943. The road was rough with gravel and we were covered in dust. We were fortunate to be able to travel in the back of a truck, which was taking oil from Shiraz to Bushehr. The bumpy road made the truck list from side to side and many of us suffered 'sea-sickness' without the luxury of seeing water. The cramped conditions were very difficult, but it was certainly a more favourable alternative than travelling by mule or horse. Javad encouraged me to close my eyes and rest, but the thought of the truck rolling off the road was sufficient to keep my eyes wide open no matter how tired I was.

When we had travelled high into the mountains, the weather became bitterly cold. We stopped at Dasht Arjen for breakfast and an opportunity to rest after the long trip. We were served hot leavened bread and a bowl of soup. It was warm and served to quell our hunger very well. Although we were only 300 kilometres from Shiraz, I felt as though we were in another country. The children who roamed around the village had fair skin and blue eyes and were dressed in colourful Turkish dresses. These children were from the Ghasghai tribe, one of the four great nomadic tribes of Iran. As he was finishing his breakfast, our driver spoke about the distance to the next city of Koziroon and said that he would have to drive much faster when we reached the edge of the lion-hunting grounds. I looked to Javad with a sense of fear and foreboding. He was calm and reassuring and said to me, 'Don't worry, my dear, not many lions are left. Maybe there are plenty of leopards, boar and deer, definitely antelopes, many wolves, foxes and hundreds of goats and thousands of rabbits – but not many lions.'

I smiled at his wry sense of humour. I wondered how other travellers on foot and shepherds could travel these parts without being afraid. Javad said that he never thought of this route from Shiraz to Bushehr in that light. With a conviction in his voice that I would come to appreciate as the deepest of faiths, he said that the path we were following had been blessed by the Báb and that he wanted to walk in the Báb's footsteps and follow the trail He had left behind. I looked into Javad's eyes and felt moved by the depth of his feelings for the Báb.

As we prepared to leave, Javad asked the driver if he might walk up the mountains that were in front of us. The driver said that he would often ask the men to walk the routes so that the truck would have enough power to reach the top. The treacherous mountain path had witnessed many tragedies, and as Javad and the other men began to walk up the path, I prayed for their safety and ours. When I opened my eyes later, I saw that the landscape had changed entirely. We had left the mountains behind us and were in the middle of pastures filled with red poppies, yellow asters, forget-me-nots and camomile. There were fruit trees that I had never seen before. It was a tapestry of colour and texture, which could surely only have been heaven.

Javad took his seat again on the truck and told me that his walk in the mountains with the other men had been most enjoyable and uneventful, unlike the last journey he had made through these parts when he had gone to visit his sister. Javad explained that on his return journey to Shiraz he had stopped to rest after lunch and lay on a rug in the sun. Half an hour later he awoke to find several hunters gathered around staring curiously at him. They told him that they had seen a miracle with their own eyes. A gigantic and ferocious leopard had escaped them as they tried to hunt it. They tracked the leopard to find it next to Javad, who was fast asleep. The men were too afraid to shoot the leopard in case they shot Javad by mistake. They watched the leopard marching up and down beside Javad's body. It smelt him from head to toe several times, then walked off leaving Javad alone, and was shot only a few metres down the road. The hunters thought Javad to be a very lucky man and that the leopard had shown no interest because he didn't move. Other people thought Javad was a holy man and that God had saved him.

At Borazjan, 60 kilometres before Bushehr, Javad and I mentioned to the driver that we wanted to see the famous ash tree of the city. According to Bahá'í oral history, the Báb had once rested under this tree, although this has not been authenticated. Not wanting to draw unnecessary attention to ourselves, we were not specific and the driver didn't stop. Years later we would visit this city and sit peacefully under the same tree. According to the villagers of Borazjan, the owner of the land where the ash tree was located asked his family to never cut down the tree because it was holy. One of his sons ignored his father's request and cut the tree down. The tree survived but the son died the next day.

3

Bushehr

Bushehr was a naturally beautiful city surrounded by deep blue waters on at least three sides. Almost every house in the city had an ocean view. Residents enjoyed the beauty of living on the Persian Gulf, and it was hard for visitors to the city not to become totally enraptured with the majesty of Bushehr's sandy beaches and beautiful vistas. In years to come, Javad, the children and I would enjoy many times at the beach watching the seagulls as they foraged for food, and the sea creatures that took refuge in the rocks and stony points of Bushehr's coast.

Its geographic location meant that the people of Bushehr came to enjoy many of the luxuries the rest of the country lived without, although when we first arrived we had to rely on a central well for water and on wood to stoke our fires. In time that would change and the houses in Bushehr would come to enjoy the luxury of gas, water and electricity. With wealthy countries such as Bahrain, Kuwait and Saudi Arabia just across the Gulf waters, Bushehr soon became a centre for imports and exports and thrived on the wealth of its Arab neighbours. With a constant flow of trade ships coming into and leaving Bushehr's port, and a steady economy to support this trade, the population of the city began to reflect the multiculturalism of the region around it and Javad and I soon came to enjoy the diversity.

Although we had both done the best we could to learn about Bushehr before we left Shiraz, the scarcity of town records meant that much of the history of the city had been passed down orally through generations and a lot of the detail and intricacies lost along the way. From what we could gather, it seemed that at some time around 300 AD Bushehr had served as a capital for that region of the world. The ruins of a palace 12 kilometres outside the city pointed to a majestic past of which there was little record.

Bushehr's climate was hot and humid most of the year. So close was it to the ocean that very little grew in its salty soil. In this arid climate, date palms flourished and would later become a major source of export for the region. The constant flow of ships to and from Bushehr's port was tempered by the stormy winter weather, which often saw hurricanes and thunderstorms batter the coast and lay waste to boats and livelihoods.

As soon as Javad and I arrived in Bushehr after our long journey from Shiraz we found our way to the House of the Báb. This was the warehouse where the Báb had conducted business, in an alley 100 metres from the sea. It was a two-storey house of approximately 1,300 square metres. The office from which the Báb worked was known by the Bahá'ís as Hojreh-i-Mubarak (the Blessed Room) and was in the middle of the ground floor of the warehouse. It was a room of 12 square metres, the smallest room in the whole building. In its early days, two straw mats covered the floor and an oil lamp sat in the corner of the room. Later a Persian rug, which covered the entire room, was donated by one of the Bahá'ís. On the side of the room facing the main entrance were three wooden windows with grilles. Each windowpane was made of nine pieces of coloured glass. One of these pieces had become loose and fallen, yet this glass was never replaced. Our neighbour told us that when it was too cold to open the windows, the Báb would put His hand through the hole to pay and receive money from His clients.

The main cargo entrance of the warehouse was a huge hand-crafted wooden gate with etchings of lions and leopards decorating the wood. At the top of the entrance was inscribed a verse from the Qur'án know as 'En Yakad'. At the end of the passageway leading from the cargo entrance were the windows of the Báb's office. In the middle of the warehouse yard was a small flower garden where a massive jasmine tree was covered with flowers most of the year and a bougainvillea flourished with red and purple flowers. Next to the garden was a deep salt-water well that fed an above-ground salt-water pool. As our children grew up, they would often swim in the pool under the shade of these luscious trees. A huge underground cistern collected and stored drinking water, which was piped down from the flat roofs on the top of all the warehouses to generously supply visitors, pilgrims and our family throughout the year.

When Javad and I arrived in Bushehr, we discovered to our delight that Javad's sister Sanam and her husband

Azizullah Saatchi (Shamshir Ali Shah's nephew) were already resident in the House of the Báb. We joined them as caretakers of that historic building. We learned later that, like Javad, Azizullah had learned of the Bahá'í Faith through his employer, and it was during this period that the Bahá'ís had given him the task of finding which of the warehouses had belonged to the Báb and arranging for its purchase.

After a tiresome search, Azizullah was certain that he had found the warehouse where the Báb had lived and conducted business. But not long after, an old man approached Azizullah, told him that he was mistaken and took him to the right warehouse. The old man told Azizullah that he had known of a Siyyid (a descendant of Prophet Muhammad) by the name of 'Alí-Muḥammad who had lived in this house. This old man had believed this Siyyid to be a prophet, and Azizullah was certain that he had now found the home of Siyyid 'Alí-Muḥammad – the Báb. Given the task of arranging the purchase of the property, Azizullah approached the owner of the warehouse, Mr Hafteh. Mr Hafteh, however, refused to sell the house, saying that the previous tenant (the Báb) had given him such good fortune that he was loath to sell the property. After much discussion, Mr Hafteh finally agreed that the property should belong to the Bahá'ís and arranged for its sale to a prominent Bahá'í in Bushehr. Azizullah then set about restoring the building and preparing the House to receive visitors and pilgrims alike. He employed a number of expert tradesmen and within a short period of time the two upstairs rooms of the property had been repaired. The important and delicate task of restoring the building was not without its share of difficulties. When it came time for the workmen to build the cistern under the yard, a retaining wall collapsed, injuring a number of the labourers. When Azizullah heard of the accident he was devastated and took it upon himself to compensate the workers out of his own limited financial resources. The restoration was halted until several months later when Shoghi Effendi, the Guardian of the Bahá'í Faith, sent funds for the completion of the project.

On 3 May 1940 he wrote commending Azizullah as a sincere and dedicated servant of the Holy Threshold; his hard work and constant efforts deserved praise, his service in this regard would not be forgotten and would attract eternal divine blessings and confirmations. He asked that photographs be taken of the finished restoration and sent to the Holy Land.

Azizullah, Sanam and their three children had resided in the House of the Báb for a year before Javad and I arrived. They soon became like parents to us and Azizullah was chiefly responsible for Javad realizing his full potential as an individual and shaping the way he would live his life. In many ways, Javad was very like Azizullah. They both had a strong commitment to making a difference in the world, their belief in the Bahá'í Faith was central to all they did, and they were both gentle and caring human beings. With great pride Javad took Azizullah's surname of Saatchi and began working as an apprentice in the jewellery shop that Azizullah owned.

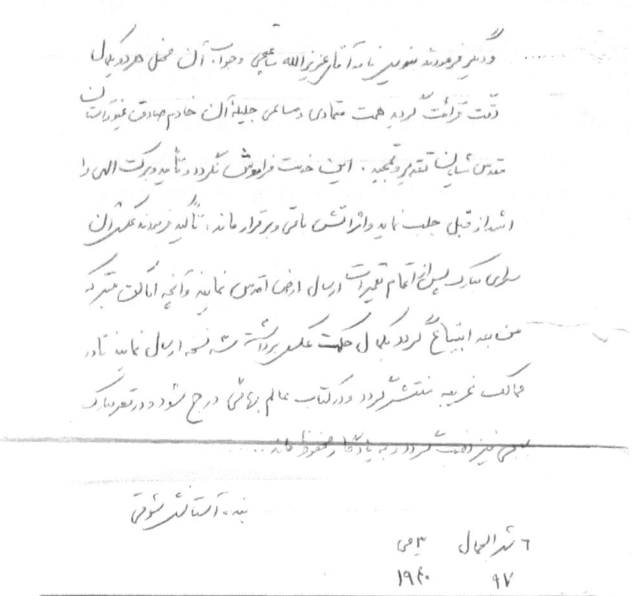

و دیگر فرمودند بنویس نامه آقا عزیزالله ساعتچی و جواب آن محفل هر دو به کمال
دقت قرائت گردید همت متمادی و مساعی جلیله آن خادم صادق عتبات
مقدس شایان تقدیر و تمجید. این خدمت فراموش نگردد و تأیید و برکت الهی را
[illegible] جلب نماید و آثارش باقی و برقرار ماند. آنچه فرمودند عکس آن
[illegible] برای اتمام تعمیرات ارسال ارض اقدس نمایند و آنچه الان متبرک
[illegible] ابتیاع گردید به کمال دقت عکس برداشته شده [illegible] ارسال نمایند تا در
ممالک غربیه منتشر گردد و در کتاب عالم بهائی درج شود و در [illegible] مبارک
[illegible] گردد و به یادگار محفوظ ماند ...

بنده آستانش شوقی

۶ شهر الجمال ۳ می
۹۷ ۱۹۴۰

Part of Shoghi Effendi's letter, May 1940, concerning the House of the Báb in Bushehr and Azizullah Saatchi's services

Azizullah, Sanam, the children and I travelled to Shiraz during what was a particularly hot summer. During our stay, Azizullah was taken ill and passed away. We were all devastated at the untimely loss of this dear man. For Sanam the grief was unbearable and she decided that she could no longer stay in Bushehr, as everything about that city reminded her of the husband she had lost. I remained in Shiraz and looked after Sanam's two younger children while she travelled back to Bushehr with her oldest daughter, and with Javad's help they packed up the family's belongings and returned to Shiraz. Sanam generously offered Javad their shop and he happily agreed to take it over, and so Javad and I returned to Bushehr, to the home we had shared with Azizullah and Sanam and their children. Javad took on the responsibility of the shop and together we became the custodians of the House of the Báb.

A little before my 14th birthday I discovered that I was pregnant with my first child. Both Javad and I were delighted to finally be having a family of our own. Two months before the baby was due to be born, I decided to return to Shiraz. I longed for the support and advice of Sanam, and also wanted to be close to better medical facilities. Too many women at that time died during childbirth and many more children died as well. I did not want to risk either my life of that of my child.

It was while I was in Shiraz that Sanam's oldest daughter Aghdas invited me to a meeting at the House of the Báb there. This house had been the scene of many great and historic events in Báhá'í history; it was a place of pilgrimage for Bahá'ís the world over, and the local Bahá'í community now used it as a centre for meetings and gatherings. Aghdas and I enrolled in a basic course about the Báhá'í Faith, given by a notable Báhá'í woman by the name of Haj <u>Kh</u>ánum Ṭúbá Afnán. When I arrived for the first class, I greeted the teacher with 'Alláh-u-Abhá', an invocation in Arabic which means 'God the All-Glorious' and which is used by Bahá'ís when they greet one another. It soon became apparent to me that this basic introduction was covering material that I had learned years before in the home of Mr Chehrenegar and also from Azizullah and Sanam. I told Mrs Afnán that for me to become a declared member of the Báhá'í Faith was a matter of formality because I had considered myself a Báhá'í since I was nine years old. On the 10th day of the course I formally declared my faith in Bahá'u'lláh as a Manifestation of God, and myself to be a Bahá'í. A greater joy I have not known. Instinctively my thoughts went to Nahid and Nasser. I wished they were there to share in the happiness and joy I felt. It had been their love and kindness which had attracted me to the Bahá'ís in the first place. In years to come, I would thank them for that gift.

I had been known until then by the name given to me at birth, Fatimih Muhammadi. My parents had named me Fatimih after the daughter of the Prophet Muhammad, and our family name of Muhammadi literally meant 'of Muhammad'. When I had first arrived in Bushehr, Azizullah said that it was appropriate for me to choose a name which reflected this new chapter in my life. He also said, if you are called Fatemeh, the local people will call you 'Fato' for short and this is not befitting for the daughter of Prophet Muhammad. If you are called, for example, Manijeh, you will be called 'Mano' for short. On the day of my formal declaration as a Bahá'í I chose the name Manijeh and took on Azizullah's family name, which Javad had proudly adopted. From then on I was known as Manijeh Saatchi. When Javad heard the news, he said 'What a wonderful year!' From then on he called me 'Mano' for short.

In returning to Shiraz for the birth of the baby I had hoped that in addition to the support of Sanam and her children I would also be able to rely on the support of my own mother. I tried on several occasions to contact her and tell her that I was pregnant but she never responded to my messages. Finally she arrived, but rather than tend to my needs as a new young mother, she began heaping insults on both Sanam and me. She said that I had been misled and that I would perish in the fire of hell for renouncing my Muslim faith. She said that my marriage to Javad, which she herself had orchestrated when I was no more than nine years old, was unlawful because he was an infidel, and that our child was illegitimate and that made me no better than the prostitutes in the street. After hours of this, Sanam asked my mother to either mind her language or leave her home. My mother was enraged and levelled the same set of insults at Sanam and her children. She said that a man had seen Aghdas and me walking towards the House of the Báb and had confronted my father with this. My father, convinced that I couldn't possibly be visiting the House of the Báb, had bet his farm that this man was lying. When it was discovered that I had indeed been going to the House of the Báb, my father honoured his foolish bet and lost the family farm. My mother now accused me of betraying my family and said that my father refused to see me ever again. With that, she stormed out of Sanam's house and left me with my newborn son Bijan, alone as I had always been.

I was 14 years old, I had been married for less than six

years, I had given birth to a son and through all of this I had neither the support of my mother nor the rest of my family. The only support I received was from the Bahá'ís, who showed me compassion and respect and welcomed me as my parents had refused to do. The thought that my son would grow up not knowing his grandparents and that they would not see this beautiful baby was more painful than I can describe. I looked at Bijan sleeping quietly. I cried uncontrollably. My life felt empty.

After a month in Shiraz, I left Sanam and her children and went back to Bushehr where Javad was overjoyed to see us. Father and son looked very alike. We were now a very young family. With the help of neighbours I soon learned how to look after Bijan and busied myself with his needs, the routine of the house and the care of the House of the Báb. Not long afterwards, the only other Báhá'í in Bushehr left the city, and Javad and I became the entire adult Bahá'í community of Bushehr. In the absence of other Bahá'ís we filled the various responsibilities of the local Báhá'í administration as cooks, cleaners, teachers, gardeners, secretaries and bookkeepers. Although we were both still so young, we embraced this immense responsibility with honour and determination. We had each other, our son and above all our faith. We had everything we needed.

When Bijan was three years old, my second son Bahram was born. Soon after, Bijan became seriously ill and we travelled often to Shiraz so that he could undergo various tests and treatments. As he grew older the neighbourhood children would make fun of him. Bijan was in and out of hospital for months on end, and when it came time for him to start school he was naturally behind the other children in his knowledge and ability. His teachers thought that he was disabled. Instead of catering to his special learning needs, they merely kept him in the lower grades and eventually he fell so far behind his age group that the school said he was too old to be in primary school. We had no alternative but to keep him home. With Bijan's illness and the responsibilities of the family, I felt my energy drain away more and more as the years passed. When Bahram became ill with pneumonia, I longed for the help and support of my mother but knew better than to ask for it.

Bijan was six and Bahram was three when our first daughter Farideh was born. She weighed just over a kilogram at birth and was jaundiced. She spent nearly a year on medication. And in 1955 our second daughter Fereshteh, Fere for short, was born. She was a healthy, bubbly baby and both Javad and I were relieved that she was in such good health. When Fere was two, Farideh also was taken ill. With three other children to look after, I felt I needed my mother's help. I sent a message to my mother asking that she come to help me. She sent a message in reply saying that she would look after Fere in Shiraz but that as our house was a house of heretics she refused to set foot in it.

I struggled as best I could with Bijan, Bahram, Farideh and Fere and soon became pregnant with our fifth child. Two months before our third daughter, Fahimeh, was born, I fell off a ladder and broke my hand, leg and ribs.

The doctors were certain that either the baby or I would die and asked Javad to choose which one they should save. When he chose me and I chose the baby, the hospital refused to get involved. They sent me home and it was only with the help of a naturopath and home remedies that I survived through to the birth of the baby. When Fahimeh was born with a broken hip, my mother did at last come to Bushehr and take Fere back to Shiraz.

For two years I struggled with raising the four children while my mother looked after Fere in Shiraz. As Fere grew older, I became increasingly concerned that she receive a good education and asked my mother to return her to Bushehr. My mother agreed to return Fere to me as long as she went back to Shiraz during the summer holidays. As time passed I began to notice that when she entered the house, Fere refused to take off her shoes as was our custom. When I asked what was wrong, she said the room was *najess* – unclean. In the evening as she would get ready for bed, Fere would recite Muslim prayers and it became obvious that my mother's influence had a firm grasp on my daughter.

As time went on, Javad worked tirelessly at the shop and I looked after the children as best I could and tended to the visitors from far and near who would come to visit the House of the Báb. Fahimeh was three years old when our sixth child and third son Bahman was born. We struggled, as families of that time were known to do, with any number of childhood maladies. It was common at that time for people to have large families, particularly in rural communities, as the various diseases of the time were almost certain to claim some of the children. Despite all the illnesses and difficulties my children suffered I was fortunate that they all survived that tenuous period of childhood and grew to be teenagers. In the end, Javad and I would have nine children – seven of whom were born while we lived in the House of the Báb and a further two in another house we occupied in Bushehr. They were, according to my mother, all illegitimate, but nothing brought Javad and me greater joy than watching our children grow up.

We suffered through floods, famine and drought. When swarms of locusts plagued Bushehr and the surrounding region, leaving the crops and stores bare, we learned how to barbecue the locusts in order to survive. While the rest of the city suffered from drought, we were fortunate that Azizullah had seen fit to build a cistern under the yard of the House of the Báb. In the times of desperate drought, our neighbours would queue at the gate for water because our cistern was the only supply in town. This was the only time people conveniently chose to accept us as one of their own. Even though I knew that their friendship was out of necessity rather than a genuine acceptance of our Bahá'í family, I was still grateful for their short-term occasional friendship.

During the years we stayed at the House of the Báb, several other Bahá'í families moved to Bushehr and before long we had a thriving community again. As a Bahá'í community we busied ourselves with projects to serve the wider community, encouraging women to educate themselves and to send their children to school. By the time my children were ready for school, the city had its first primary school and the children of the city were well served by it. Our lives in Bushehr remained simple. We cooked over open fires long after people in the city were using stoves. Our children did not enjoy the luxury of toys but amused themselves with shells and stones and whatever else they could find. Their lives were not rich in a material sense but were certainly rich in the love of their parents and each other. The values which Javad and I tried to instill in our children did not come from objects and ownership, but from love and service. We did our best. Our lives were happy.

Of all our children, Bijan suffered the most. His childhood illness had left him isolated from his peers. He was often made fun of and ridiculed. He suffered from a lack of concentration and was often hyperactive. I believe that he suffered from what is known today as attention deficit disorder (ADD). His teachers and other children treated him cruelly and when he was 15 years old he decided that he wanted to meet his grandparents. Not wanting to speak ill of my parents, I didn't mention any of what had transpired between us or tell Bijan that my family had disowned me when I had became a Bahá'í. When Bijan announced he was going to travel to Shiraz, I became even more concerned for him. He seemed unsettled and said he wanted to find out more about himself. Finding work on a truck, Bijan set off for Shiraz. After some time he called us to say that he had visited my mother and had decided to stay with her for a while. I was grateful that at least he had a roof over his head and hoped that, whatever my mother might have thought of me, she would at least look after my son. At first we would hear from Bijan often and he would send boxes of fruit to us from time to time. But after a while, even this sparse contact stopped. It had been many months since he left when Bijan called me again to say that my mother had pressured him into marrying the daughter of a respected Muslim cleric. My heart broke as I realized that instead of helping Bijan to come back to his family, my mother had forced him to stay away. Bijan was married without his parents or siblings present. As a result of the influence of my mother, I lost contact with him for a long time. By the time I saw him again, he had two children. Bijan suffered throughout this time, and as a mother I suffered with him. He was hospitalized for long periods on end and our lack of contact over the years made it harder and harder to rebuild the relationship we once had.

Bushehr: views of the House of the Báb, showing the seafront

The cargo entrance, looking towards the 'Blessed Room' (Hojreh-i-Mubarak) where the Báb conducted business

Inside the chamber, showing a carpet with quotations from the Báb's Writings woven in

One of the rooms on the upper floor, with nine doors

Second room on the upper floor; here Bahá'í meetings were held

Members of the first Spiritual Assembly of Bushehr.
Left to right, standing: Azizullah Saatchi, Mr Hooshmand; seated: Mr Saif, Hossein Mahboubi, Mr Faez, Amirzadeh Salmanpoor

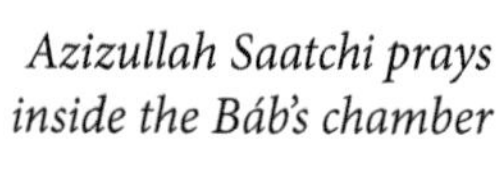

Azizullah Saatchi prays inside the Báb's chamber

4

Pilgrims

The House of the Báb in Bushehr became a significant place of pilgrimage for Bahá'ís from around the world. It was not uncommon for us to receive visitors from as far away as North America and the Pacific. Even though we had difficulties in communication, Javad and I delighted in their visits and the opportunity to offer them hospitality.

Although on most occasions these visits were hardly noticed, there were times when we had to rely on our ingenuity to bring the pilgrims safely to and from the House of the Báb. On one such occasion two African Bahá'ís, a father and son, arrived by ship at the port of Bushehr. At that time, several of the religious leaders in Iran had taken exception to the Bahá'í community. The latent persecution, which we had grown accustomed to, became more fierce and unrelenting. Many Bahá'ís had their houses attacked and their belongings destroyed. Others chose to leave Iran in fear. In Bushehr, the authorities contented themselves by posting guards around the House of the Báb and stopping anyone who tried to enter or leave the house. For months we were effectively prisoners in our own house, not allowed to leave and certainly not allowed to receive visitors. Returning from his morning walk, our neighbour, Omar, saw these two African men making inquiries at the Customs Office and struggling to make themselves understood. They were inquiring about the home of Siyyid 'Alí-Muḥammad. Omar knew immediately they must be Bahá'í pilgrims wanting to visit the House of the Báb. He offered to show them the way.

Omar and his wife, whom I called 'Objee', a term of endearment meaning 'sister', had been our neighbours since we arrived in Bushehr. Objee had helped me when I first returned from Shiraz with Bijan. Although Omar and Objee were staunch Muslims, we had always been friendly with one another. Coincidentally, they were custodians of a Muslim Holy Place in Bushehr known as 'Abbas Ali'. It was said that a holy man had once slept under the only tree in the garden of the house. Muslims would often visit to pray or light candles of remembrance around that tree. Every day Objee would clean the courtyard of the house in anticipation of the visitors who would come to pray. Both Objee and I were custodians of Holy Places and this common ground fostered a trust and respect between us.

When Omar returned to our neighbourhood with these two African Bahá'ís, he was well aware that the guards posted outside our house would never allow them to enter and that their long journey to visit the House of the Báb would be in vain. Whatever our religious differences might have been, Omar knew how important pilgrimage was in any religion, so instead of taking the African Bahá'ís to our house, he took them to his own. There he asked them to wait. It was decided that Objee would distract the guards from our house and Omar would then sneak the African Bahá'ís in through a rear entrance. Quite unexpectedly I heard Objee yelling, 'Thief! Thief!' I ran to the front of the house, genuinely believing that she had been robbed. The guards posted around the House of the Báb similarly responded to her cries and left their post to go to her aid. Amidst the commotion which followed, Omar quietly led the African Bahá'ís into the House of the Báb through a back door.

Omar stayed and watched as these two African men reverently entered the rooms which the Báb had occupied and immersed themselves in devoted prayer. It was obvious that he was moved by this display of reverent affection. He turned to me and said, 'If a new religion unifies people, why should anyone care?' Omar had put himself and his family at risk in order to assist these Bahá'í visitors and in so doing had shown that our friendship and respect for each other could overcome our differences of faith. Omar waited patiently as these African Bahá'ís prayed and then quietly led them back out the rear entrance. They stayed that evening with Omar and Objee and left the next morning to board a ship.

I would come to rely on Objee's help on another occasion, when several American Bahá'ís arrived in Bushehr and began making their way from the port to the House of the Báb. An increasing number of children gathered around them, calling out, 'Yanks! Yanks!' Despite Bushehr's isolation from the Western world, the children were quick to pick up whatever words they could. As the pilgrims approached, I could see that the number of children around them had increased and I feared that the children would follow the American Bahá'ís into the house and cause damage. Unsure of what to do, I consulted my wise old friend Objee. When I said I needed her help, Objee began to laugh, no doubt remembering our last collaboration for the African visitors. I continued, 'Objee, Bahá'ís are here and hundreds of children are following them. What do you think I should do?' Objee smiled wryly and simply said, 'Leave it to me.' As the American Bahá'ís and the growing number of children reached the House of the Báb, Objee went to the balcony, and with a loud voice began to yell, 'Thief! Thief!' just as she had done when the African pilgrims had visited. The children, as children are wont to do, thought that catching a thief was far more interesting than following the 'Yanks' and their attention was soon diverted from the American visitors.

I quickly ushered the visitors into the house. After introducing them to the children who were playing in the yard, we went into our living quarters and shared lunch together. Javad explained that the sweet grapefruits that we were eating had been the Báb's favourite fruit and that when the Báb travelled from Bushehr to Mecca on pilgrimage his faithful Ethiopian servant Mubarak had carried a large basket of this fruit to the ship so that the Báb could enjoy it during his travels. After lunch, we took our visitors downstairs to the rooms which the Báb had occupied and left them there to pray. On the way back upstairs I noticed some very confused children in the alley, wondering what had happened to the 'Yanks' and the thief. When our visitors had finished their prayers,

I quietly went and told Objee that the pilgrims had finished and were ready to go back to their ship. Once again the children were distracted and the pilgrims quietly left.

Among many things, I was grateful that our presence at the House of the Báb in Bushehr and the steady flow of Western and Eastern pilgrims gave my children a sense of belonging to a worldwide family. Whatever taunts they were subjected to at school, they had experiences that other children could only dream of. We would welcome pilgrims of every race and creed, Bahá'ís from countries we had never heard of, all humble and devoted believers in a nascent world faith. That meant having the same vision for the world, the same spiritual principles, and the same universal value system. They would come speaking only a few words of Persian, if that, but yet we communicated happily and easily with our hearts. The children would gladly give up whatever meagre provisions we had in order to see that the pilgrims were looked after, and watch in awe as these Western Bahá'ís would enter the rooms of the Báb with a reverence which words fail to adequately describe. We all clearly understood what Bahá'u'lláh meant when he wrote that 'the world is but one country and mankind its citizens'. This was our vision, and we shared it with people the world over.

Despite the great joy that the visits of the pilgrims brought, I would always remind the children not to speak of these visits at school. They were careful not to share news about the Bahá'í activities. Above all, we were worried that if people discovered the significance of the House to the Bahá'ís, they would be intent on causing damage. Our secrecy was not only to protect the children but also to protect our young Faith. Despite our attempts, the children would nevertheless suffer at the hands of their classmates. Farideh would come home from school crying that the other children would call her names and say that she lived in that 'bad' house that men visited. The implication for onlookers was that because the majority of the pilgrims we received were men, it must be a house of ill repute.

One day, when I was pregnant and on my way home after a medical appointment, Bijan found me and said that Bahram had gone missing. Bahram had always been a brave child and was not easily scared, but on this occasion one of the other children had threatened to kill him because he was a Bahá'í. Several Bahá'ís gathered at our home that evening and, as there was still no sign of Bahram, they each went in different directions looking for him. We searched the wharf, the boats and the side alleys, but to no avail. As night fell I became increasingly scared and worried for his well-being. It was unthinkable that children could threaten each other because of a prejudice that their parents had instilled in them. We searched long into the night and there was no trace of Bahram. As it happened, Bahram had seen the group of people looking for him and had feared that they were going to kill him. He had climbed a 60-metre high crane and hidden there. We searched until mid-morning the following day and became exhausted. Then, by chance, someone noticed an arm dangling from the compartment of the crane. Climbing up, they found Bahram fast asleep and precariously close to the edge of the balcony. Although our children suffered more than they should have, with gentle coaxing and constant reassurance from Javad and me, they always returned to school despite their protests.

The harassment was never confined to just the children. Over the years we became accustomed to the strange looks and suspicious nature of the people we met in the street. The port authorities would constantly shine their spotlights on the House of the Báb and watch our every move. When I complained, I was told that they were merely watching the ships as they pulled into the port and the House just happened to be in the way. On one occasion, as I was returning from grocery shopping, I noticed that a man was following me home. As I stopped to buy food, he would stop. When I continued he would follow. He followed me through the market. As we neared the house I heard him calling out to me, 'Miss! Miss!' After he had called several times I turned to confront him. I explained that because I was married it would be more appropriate for him to be calling, 'Mrs! Mrs!' and asked what his business was with me. He introduced himself as being a member of SAVAK (the Secret Service) and indicated he had some questions for me. I noticed then that he held a small tape recorder in his hand. I explained to him that he was a stranger to me and that before I spoke with him any further I wished to pray. He didn't object and I recited one of the prayers revealed by the Báb for protection. He waited as I finished and then went on to recite a second prayer. It was important for me to convey a message on this tape that I was religious and a woman of principle. When I finished, this man said that he knew that my husband worked very hard in his shop but often did not earn much money. He said that he would give me a sum of money if I would tell him what happened in the House of the Báb.

I explained to him the Bahá'í Faith was a global religion and that Bahá'ís believed in the oneness of God, the oneness of religion and the oneness of humanity. I pointed out to him that Bahá'ís believed that there was only one God even though He might be called by different names, and that as such we respected all the world's religions as coming from this one source. I went on to say that Bahá'ís believed that Bahá'u'lláh was the most recent in a line of Messengers coming from God and that this process of divine guidance would continue. I reassured him that Bahá'ís were peaceful people and that we didn't involve ourselves in partisan politics and that we were obedient and loyal to government, as any citizen should be.

After listening to my explanation, he said quite unconsciously that it seemed Bahá'ís had important work to do and that our non-involvement in politics would make it easier for us to focus on what we wanted to achieve. Once he had verbalized this sentiment he went on to offer me double the amount of money if I would tell him what went on in the House of the Báb. I was surprised that after my lengthy explanation he did not believe me. I reiterated that I was telling him the truth and this seemed to make him more agitated. He accused me of being brainwashed and said that I was using words that I surely did not know the meaning of. After a barrage of insults he promptly turned his tape recorder off and disappeared into the crowd. I never did find out who had listened to that tape, but I felt certain that the situation for the Bahá'ís was bound to get worse before it got better.

5

The Destruction of the House of the Báb

In 1966 the provincial government of Bushehr decided that the wharf needed to be enlarged in order to expand the capabilities of the port city. The implication of this decision was that the warehouses on the eastern side of the port would be demolished. Both we and our neighbours were greatly surprised by this announcement, particularly as it was well known that the deeper water would be found on the western side of the existing wharf, and that the lack of any buildings and infrastructure on that side would make it a much more viable option. Although we were never able to prove our theory, both Javad and I were convinced that the motivation of the authorities was not to increase the capacity of the wharf but rather to ensure the destruction of the House of the Báb.

Two months after this announcement, the Empress of Iran, Farah Pahlavi, arrived in Bushehr for the naming ceremony of the wharf. It was to be named after her son Reza. With the arrival of the royal entourage, it seemed certain that it was only a matter of time before the House of the Báb would be bulldozed to make room for the new infrastructure. Following the naming ceremony, our family gathered in the rooms that had been occupied by the Báb and prayed that somehow this Holy Place would be spared from destruction. The rooms in which we prayed held a special significance for Bahá'ís around the world. And for Javad and me it had been the greatest honour to serve the Bahá'í community as custodians of the Holy Place.

Our worst fears were realized at dawn when the bulldozers and other machinery arrived to tear down the buildings. As they moved closer, Javad was intent on stopping them; he said he would lie down in front of the bulldozers. He was prepared to protect the House of the Báb with his life. The operators of the machinery ignored our pleas and protests and continued with their work day after day. When it became clear that Javad would not relent in his protest, the workers stopped temporarily, threatening to take Javad to court for obstructing the legitimate demolition of the buildings. Our neighbours and friends tried in vain to get Javad to move out of the way of the machinery. Finally, the members of the local Spiritual Assembly of the Bahá'ís of Bushehr came and spoke to Javad. They explained that Bahá'ís did not worship buildings and that the essence of our Faith was our belief and worship of God through His Messengers and that it was time for us to show detachment and accept whatever was the will of God.

As the bulldozers came closer to the warehouse we occupied, I sent the children to Shiraz to be with Sanam. Javad and I watched in horror, as first the exterior walls of the warehouse were demolished and later the rooms that the Báb had occupied. As the sun broke on that dreadful day over the ruins of the House of the Báb, the devastation became apparent and Javad mournfully said, 'Mano, we are finished.' He was so traumatized that nothing else seemed to matter to him. I remembered back to the day we had arrived in Bushehr so many years before. Javad had been totally consumed with devotion and longing to serve the Bahá'í Faith. His greatest honour had been to be the custodian of this House of the Báb. For years we had prepared the rooms which the Báb had occupied to receive pilgrims from around the world. Now, with reckless abandon, this holy spot was a mere pile of rubble. The demolition of the House of the Báb in 1967 was one of the saddest events we would ever experience.

As the days passed, Javad and I busied ourselves with finding other accommodation for the family. Muslims refused to rent us a house because they claimed that no one else would rent it again if we left the property. This was the fate of any house where untouchables lived. In the end we were forced to live in an old three-storey house which had been vacant for some time. This house belonged to the family doctor. Although it was far from suitable, we soon realized that we would have to make do with whatever we could find. The front of the house had collapsed, the floors were damp and rotted, and all manner of snakes and vermin infested the basement. We were restricted to the three bedrooms on the floor above the ground floor. We used the floor above that for Bahá'í meetings. Although we had electricity, there was no plumbing, and the toilet consisted of a hole in the ground. None of the children was brave enough to venture to the toilet alone. Every time nature called, there would be a line of children waiting in turn so as not to be by themselves.

Javad soon became very popular in our new neighbourhood. I often heard children calling, 'Hello, Mr Saatchi, Hello, Mr Saatchi,' as he left the house. He always had sweets and small coins in his pocket to share with them. Sometimes he would come home empty-handed from shopping, having given what little we could afford to those less fortunate. Gradually men started going to Javad's shop to ask questions or discuss religious issues. They called him 'the Bábí prophet' even though Javad assured them he was simply a man like them who wanted to learn.

We struggled as we had done before, but with the added heartbreak of knowing that the House of the Báb was no longer. I busied myself with looking after nine children in conditions which were difficult at best of times. We had no tap water, so I would wash loads of clothes each day by hand and hope that the sun would come out. There was no refrigeration so I would have to go to the market each day for food. By the time breakfast was finished, it was time to prepare lunch for when the children would be home from school. No sooner was lunch finished than preparations would begin for dinner.

Amidst the routine of our lives, Javad would often visit neighbouring communities to meet with other Bahá'ís. It was not surprising for him to return home with one or two orphaned children. We would look after them until we could find someone to care for them permanently. Many nights we would have just bread and yoghurt for dinner, yet we were grateful. Javad had a small income from repairing watches and clocks, but the money was barely enough to feed the children and to keep them clothed. We did without many basic necessities, much less luxuries. We did not own much furniture. The children would sleep three or four to a room on whatever bedding we could put on the floor. A Persian rug donated by a Bahá'í for the house became the family blanket on freezing winter nights. The one luxury we did allow ourselves was a small transistor radio. Javad and I would listen to the BBC world news each day until one day our youngest daughter Faranak accidentally dropped the radio while trying to see the people who were talking inside it.

Because life was difficult, our children focused more on their studies and education. I am sure part of their motivation was that they did not want to be poor when they grew up. My daughters had one toy between them, an old rag doll, and would take it in turn to play with it. They would often use their imagination to dream up new games and stories to keep them amused. Sometimes they would turn their pillows into rabbits by tying string around the middle to make a body and in the two corners to make ears. They would happily play with the neighbourhood children. For the most part they seemed to be spared the taunts and insults which pervaded the school grounds.

The younger children did not face as much difficulty as the older ones, because the primary-school teachers seemed kinder and more tolerant. The school policy was that children born to non-Muslim families were not allowed to attend Arabic/Quranic scripture classes. When they insisted on attending they were given only a pass grade at best of times, irrespective of their knowledge or ability. Our fourth child Fere always received the highest marks in all her subjects except these classes. Yet, thanks to Javad and the teacher of her Bahá'í classes, Mrs Rouhani, she showed such remarkable ability in reading the Qur'án that she was selected from the 800 students in the school to read the Qur'án at the beginning of each school day. Despite her obvious ability, she was never given the top grade.

6

Fere and Abbas

In 1973 Fere graduated from high school at the age of 18 and also won first prize in a literary competition for an article she wrote on peace. She appeared on television and on the front page of the local paper and was subsequently offered a place at the Pahlavi University in Shiraz. She was one of the first girls from Bushehr to attend university. Javad and I were certainly the proudest parents, feeling that our years of hard work and struggle had paid off.

In early 1975, Fere met her future husband Abbas, who was also studying at Pahlavi University. Seven months later, Abbas won an overseas scholarship to complete his Master's degree in electronic engineering. Thus the question arose as to what was to become of their relationship. It was clear to both Javad and me that they seemed compatible as a couple and Fere had assured us that Abbas loved her very much. She said that on one occasion Abbas took her with him to a doctor's appointment and showing her his heart on the ultrasound said, 'It's yours! It's calling your name!' Neither Abbas nor Fere felt ready for marriage, yet at the same time it was inappropriate for them to have a long engagement. Quite apart from the fact that Bahá'í law permitted only a 95-day engagement period, Javad and I had always believed that if two people genuinely wanted to get married then they should make a commitment to each other and not 'hedge their bets' with a long engagement that could then later be broken. At first Abbas took our disapproval of a long engagement as meaning that we disapproved of his plans to study overseas, and that we wanted him to remain in Iran and forfeit whatever adventure and opportunity might present itself. He soon realized however that we were talking from experience and only had their best interests at heart.

It was clear to both Javad and me that Fere was very much in love with Abbas, to the point that she was even prepared to give up her university studies to follow him to England. Up to that time Fere had received several proposals of marriage. In each case she had refused, saying that she wanted to complete her university degree. In this case, however, she was prepared to sacrifice even that. In the lengthy discussions that took place over this period, Fere made it clear that she was prepared to make a commitment to Abbas. She told Javad, 'When we don't believe in excessive freedom and infidelity, when we don't believe in trying out different partners, I might as well commit myself to him.' She said, 'It is unlikely that my heart would have the same feeling for somebody else.' She said, 'I will never fall in love again so it will be better to commit myself to this relationship and give the seed a chance to become a tree.' Javad was concerned about Fere leaving university, but after consulting with her professors, it was apparent to him that it would be possible for Fere to continue her studies in England.

When Fere and Abbas asked for our consent to marry, we gladly gave it, asking that Abbas consider only two requests from us. The first was that Fere should be given every opportunity to finish her studies overseas; the second, that they consult fairly and equally on all matters concerning their life together. We believed that Fere had a right to be treated as an equal partner in marriage and that our job as her parents was to ensure that this happened. Abbas not only supported our ideas but also said that he wholeheartedly believed that men and women should have the same opportunity to reach their full potential. I was also concerned that by moving so far from her family and the environment that she was used to, Fere would feel lonely and out of place. Abbas reassured us that Fere would have every happiness and success. With the family gathered round, Abbas and Fere were married in a modest ceremony at the end of October 1975 and left for England that December.

Despite the distance, Fere would write to us regularly, sharing with us all the experiences that England brought with it. She wrote that not long after she and Abbas had settled into their apartment, a young man knocked on the door and asked her how many bottles of milk he should deliver. Fere was sure that he was joking because milk delivery did not happen in Iran. She said the first number that came to her mind – two. To her surprise he went to his van and returned with two bottles of milk. It was not long before Fere asked me to send her recipes for making cheese and yoghurt. Clearly the milk supply was getting to be quite plentiful. Among other things, Fere would write about the beauty of England and the generosity of the people, whom she would describe as 'all blonde' and looking alike. Coming from Bushehr and later Shiraz, the lush surroundings of the English countryside were refreshingly different. And coming from a country where from childhood she had been taunted for being a Bahá'í, I am sure Fere felt grateful to live in a country where people were genuinely friendly and generous.

It was a challenge for Fere to begin her studies again in a different language. She struggled with grammatical differences that her lecturers found rather amusing. Fere would often say 'he' when she meant 'she' and vice versa. She would explain that in Persian there were no personal pronouns and that everyone was referred to as 'it'. Despite spending many long hours in the library Fere often wrote that it was simply impossible for her to catch up with the work that she had to do. The cultural adjustment was also difficult, and it took some time for Abbas and Fere to acquaint themselves with the local customs and culture. Being invited to a colleague's home for 'tea', both Abbas and Fere anticipated receiving a cup of tea and made sure that they had their dinner before they left. When they arrived they discovered that 'tea' was in fact roast beef and Yorkshire pudding. Amidst the daily adventures that this new country provided, Fere and Abbas both looked forward to their visits home. We came to expect their return during their winter holidays.

In 1978, after two years of postgraduate studies in England, Abbas came back to Iran to fulfil his employment contract with the Government while Fere remained in England to finish her degree in food and management. Abbas was offered a job by the Iranian Atomic Energy Establishment and was posted to Bushehr. We were delighted to have our son-in-law working in such a prestigious establishment. He had a very comfortable lifestyle, living in a nice house with his father, Ziaullah. Javad and Ziaullah were very good friends, so we would visit their house very often. We were grateful that our son-in-law had managed to establish himself so well.

But in 1979 with the Iranian Revolution, after Abbas had worked for the Atomic Energy Establishment for almost a year and a half, he was informed that as a Bahá'í his position within the company was precarious. He could either accept immediate dismissal or wait to have his contract severed at a later date. Abbas decided to stay, hoping that the situation would improve and that he would be able to retain his position and benefits. In the meantime, Fere was under a lot of pressure in London. She was missing Abbas and was worried about her family. Deciding that she would risk the deteriorating conditions, she returned home for the winter holidays. When she arrived, she found the country in chaos. Martial law had been imposed. In the capital, Tehran, the situation was nearing crisis point. After waiting 24 hours in the airport, Fere at last boarded a flight to Bushehr. Her joy at seeing Abbas and the family was soon replaced by a sense of shock when she realized that the family was being systematically persecuted for being Bahá'ís. The homes of many relatives had been looted and burned, and the shop belonging to Abbas's father had suffered the same fate. Although originally planning to stay for only a month, Fere ended up staying for three, because she was unable to get a flight out of Iran. Abbas and Fere made daily trips to the airport in the hope of finding a seat, and at last Fere boarded a flight for London via Frankfurt. When she arrived in London she realized that her luggage had been misdirected. The suitcases were never recovered; she lost all her clothes and personal items and also her textbooks and course notes. This setback meant that she had to repeat two of her subjects. In the meantime Fere also discovered she was pregnant.

Not long after this, Abbas was dismissed from the Atomic Energy Establishment and lost his home, furniture and source of income. Far away, Fere was expecting their first child and growing increasingly concerned for her husband and family. She would later tell us that year was one of the worst of her life. The new Iranian Government had suspended her scholarship because she was a Bahá'í. Letters she sent to Abbas failed to arrive. It was only the kindness of her English friends and the support of the Dean of the college that allowed her to remain in London. With assistance from the British Government, Fere stayed and finished her degree, but when it came time for her to find accommodation outside the college, she found it difficult to rent an apartment because people were scared to rent property to Iranians. Finally Fere resorted to telling people she was from Bushehr, in the hope that they would leave it at that and not ask anything further.

Meanwhile, in Iran, Abbas was struggling along with

many other Bahá'ís to find work. The Islamic regime of Ayatollah Khomeini had declared that Bahá'ís were heretics and, as such, enjoyed neither rights nor privilege under the law. Realizing that his future was not going to be in Iran, Abbas reluctantly decided to return to England, but even then he was forced to pay 50,000 tumans (10,000 US dollars) at Tehran airport in order to leave the country. A few weeks later, he telephoned to tell us that our grandson Dana had been born. In the midst of these difficulties and persecutions, the birth of this boy gave all of us a reason for rejoicing; it allowed Fere and Abbas some moments of respite from the financial constraints and uncertain future they faced. Abbas tried to find work, but did not have a permit to work in England. Fere did have a permit to work but was busy looking after a newborn baby. It was not long before they found themselves with nowhere to live. Unable to return to Iran for fear of religious persecution, they applied for refugee status in England or to be accepted as refugees in another country. After many applications and long periods of waiting, Abbas, Fere and Dana were accepted by the Australian Government and arrived in Australia in December 1980.

7

Revolution and Persecution

With the triumph of the Islamic Revolution in Iran in 1979, the sporadic persecution of the Bahá'ís which had characterized much of its history became systematized. Since 1979, over 200 Bahá'ís have been executed for their belief, while hundreds more have been imprisoned. Their key to freedom has always been the unconscionable demand that they deny their faith. Tens of thousands have been deprived of work, pensions, businesses and educational opportunities. The property of Bahá'ís, their holy places and cemeteries, have been confiscated and destroyed, and the 300,000-strong Bahá'í community in Iran, the largest religious minority in that country, have been designated as 'non-persons' under the law and are afforded neither rights nor protection.

These were the conditions and fears under which we lived as Iran shifted from a constitutional monarchy with some strong religious factions to a country governed in every respect by Islamic law. We feared not only attacks by the authorities but also reprisals from ordinary citizens, who had been led to believe that the Bahá'ís presented a religious and moral threat to the fabric of Iran.

Among this fear and intimidation, there were those

who still showed us some support and compassion. Years before when I was breast-feeding Bahram, a young mother had come to me with her child. She was depressed and ashamed that she was not producing enough milk to feed it. As was common in those days, I agreed to breast-feed her child for her. Javad and I came to love this boy and would refer to him as our 'foster son'. We delighted as he grew into a fine young man. When the persecution of the Bahá'ís began in earnest, this boy, now a young man, came to see us. He had heard that our property had been confiscated and that our family, like all other Bahá'ís, was facing intense persecution at the hands of the clergy. He was incensed at this blatant hatred and prejudice and said that he would gladly 'take care' of whoever it was that was causing us this trouble. He knew, though, that violence and revenge went against everything that we believed as Bahá'ís and that we would lead by example by being peaceful and law-abiding citizens. He was not alone in his support. Through those most difficult times we would continue to find those that were confused and ashamed that their Government and their clergy were persecuting a peace-loving community.

Farideh, my eldest daughter, and her husband Parviz were also victims of prejudice and discrimination in the early days of the Revolution. Both Farideh and Parviz held senior positions with the National Health Department. They were sure that their years of service would afford them some security, even in these troubled times. Parviz was reading the staff bulletin one day when he read a notice regarding a 'campaign of opposition to

Islam carried out by American and Israeli spies'. The article outlined strategies for 'cleansing' the system of such agents. With the world centre of the Bahá'í Faith being in present-day Israel, Bahá'ís were often accused of being spies for Israel, which was as far from the truth as was possible. A brief history lesson would have shown that at the time the Bahá'í holy places were established in the Holy Land, it was part of the Ottoman Empire. The creation of the State of Israel took place some 80 years after Bahá'u'lláh was first exiled there. Concerned that this article might be an indirect reference to Bahá'ís, Parviz asked his superiors to clarify what the article meant. It was then that he was told that his services in the Health Department were no longer needed. Stunned, Parviz called Farideh, who worked one floor above him in the office, only to find that Farideh too had been dismissed. They left together without any payment for the last month of work and certainly no mention of any form of superannuation or termination payments. Most of the people who worked with Farideh and Parviz were confused and disturbed by their dismissal, but were too frightened to protest.

It was not long before their driving licences were not renewed and their applications for business permits were continually denied. Farideh and Parviz had also thought of leaving Iran, but their applications for passports were always denied. Farideh sadly remarked one day, 'They don't want us here and they won't let us go anywhere else. I don't think they know what they want any more.'

With no income and no prospect of employment, it

was not long before Farideh began to lose her self-esteem and self-worth. She had always worked, and I had gladly helped her by looking after the children. Both Parviz and Farideh were hospitalized for stress-induced ailments. Parviz was trying to run a business in the open market. Although people were quite happy to sell him goods, no one would buy from him. He was, after all, a Bahá'í. I often asked God to help me understand the significance of this suffering. Bahá'ís always approached their work with integrity and commitment. The Bahá'í vision of creating a better world found expression in everything we did. For many years before, Bahá'ís had been seen as an asset to any company or government department. Now, they were summarily discharged and their lives thrown into chaos. It was difficult to understand.

Farideh and Parviz went from one city to another, trying different business ideas that always left them with less money than when they started. They eventually settled in Isfahan, where a family member had offered Parviz a job. They stayed there for close to a year before my husband Javad became ill and they returned to Bushehr. At around the same time the Revolutionary Guards attacked our home and seized our belongings. Among the things they took was the complete record of the Bahá'í community. This provided the Revolutionary Guards with a list whereby they could identify members of the Bahá'í community throughout the region.

Javad's illness that necessitated Parviz and Farideh's return resulted from the second time he was attacked on his way home from the shop. The first incident had happened one night a few weeks earlier. For the past few years he had been walking to his shop and back again to stay healthy and save money on paying taxis. He had sometimes been late on previous occasions after a meeting of the Local Spiritual Assembly or a Committee, but never that late. That night there was no Assembly meeting, nor was he attending a committee meeting. The whole country was going through a revolution and it was not safe to be out late. I was very worried about him. I talked to Bahram. He was worried too. Eventually, Bahram found some courage, got on his motorcycle and went looking for his father. Now I was worried about both of them, and I said some prayers, hoping to see them soon. After a very long one hour, they both arrived. They looked intensely horrified. Bahram said he had found his Dad lying on the ground in the middle of the lane shivering, scared, lethargic and feeling unsafe. He also said that his Dad had not wanted to go to hospital as he was worried about making a scene. He did not want to talk about it in the lane, he just wanted to come home. So Bahram brought him home. Crying helplessly, I listened to what Bahram said, just happy to see them alive.

After several hours of nursing Javad started to talk slowly. He told me, 'The problem was with religion, because I had not stopped misleading people. There were a group of men in uniform asking different questions and accusing me of things I had not done. My answer was clear, I had not misled anyone because I did not believe I was saying anything misleading. They punched me and threw me to the ground, kicked me and said that because of my protest and disgusting belief in the Bahá'í Faith I would no longer be able to go to work. Then they said, if you keep teaching Muslims you will be arrested, charged with apostasy, misleading and evangelism to Muslims.'

The second attack was much worse than the first. Although Javad lost consciousness for some moments, he insisted that he felt fine and did not want to go to the hospital. Feeling a little better in the morning, he went to town to attend to some urgent business, but on his return collapsed at the door. I ran to him, distressed and helpless. As I reached him the delivery from the grocery store arrived and I begged the driver to take us to the only hospital in Bushehr. As we arrived in the emergency room, the staff refused to treat Javad, saying he would recover and they had to give priority to the young soldiers wounded in Iran–Iraq war. I could see that Javad was in excruciating pain. After I pleaded with them, they at last gave Javad some medication that eased the pain.

While we were waiting, the emergency room filled with young soldiers who had been injured when their ship was attacked in the Persian Gulf. This influx of new patients meant that Javad was dropped from the list for treatment. I was asked to take him home. I was horrified that they would discriminate on age, but then I realized that not only were we facing persecution, we were doing so during a time of revolution and war. The war with Iraq had been going on for two years. Many doctors and other professionals had fled Iran. Those who remained at the hospitals were often no more than medical students. Javad was nearly 60 years old and clearly not able to defend his country on the battlefield. What did I expect? Realizing that Javad would receive little treatment in Bushehr, I asked for an ambulance to take him to Shiraz, a four-hour drive, in the hope that a larger hospital with more staff and facilities might be able to assist us. The staff flatly refused. I reminded the nurse that our daughter and son-in-law had worked for the Health Department for 20 years, surely that must count for something. It made no difference. In desperation I went to the authority offices in search of a neighbour who worked there, thinking that he might be able to help. Finally the manager came. In desperation I told him everything – that I was a Bahá'í, my husband was a Bahá'í and that he was dying; that the hospital refused to treat him; that I was appealing to their sense of fairness and humanity to please lend me a means of transport so that I could take Javad to Shiraz.

To the amazement of the hospital staff I returned with a vehicle. Seeing that I was determined to take Javad to a hospital in Shiraz, the staff agreed that I use the ambulance and soon we were on our way. I sat next to Javad, exhausted. Javad had his right hand on his heart. I reached out for his left hand. An hour into the trip Javad's condition worsened and I felt he had no pulse. The driver refused to take him any further and we returned to the hospital in Bushehr. There the doctor gave him another injection and I begged him to hang on for the sake of the children and for me. The minute I said it, I felt guilty. Why should I burden Javad further by making him think that he was letting us down? I rephrased my words. I told Javad not to worry about us, that the children and I would be fine. Our marriage of many years had led to a deep love and profound respect. I wished I could take his place and bear his suffering. I loved him so much that I could not imagine life without him. I held his hand in mine and in a voice that I hoped sounded calm I said, 'Javad, I know you will make it. Please try for me.'

The doctors had said that Javad could stay overnight, but that I had to leave because I was not allowed to stay in the men's ward. I paced the floor of the women's ward that night, praying and occasionally checking on Javad. He was receiving medication intravenously and managed to sleep despite the pain. On occasions it would seem to me that he had a mystical expression on his face. In the morning, we left for Shiraz.

When Farideh and Parviz heard that Javad had collapsed and been taken to hospital, they came to Shiraz immediately. Bahram had worked for an American pharmaceutical company and knew some of the hospital staff. He tried as best he could to get some help for his father. Although Javad felt better, he seemed to sense that he was dying. He told us that the hour had come and that it was a remarkable occasion in his life. When he was awake, he was chanting prayers. Amidst our grief and sadness, Javad was happy. He reminded me of what Bahá'u'lláh wrote regarding death, 'I have made death a messenger of joy to thee, wherefore dost thou grieve?' Javad asked me to be happy and to live in peace. He asked us not to wear black at his funeral or afterwards, but to rejoice in his life, fully lived, and to find comfort in the knowledge that he was in a better place. He made me promise that I would remain strong and calm, and set a good example for the children. With the members of the family gathered around, he told the children that I was a strong woman with convictions and intuition and the spiritual qualities of love and service. He asked them to look up to me and to love me for his sake. He then asked Farideh to read aloud a paragraph he had copied from a Bahá'í book regarding union in the next world. I felt that Javad looked right through me while Farideh read, 'According to Bahá'u'lláh the soul retains its individuality and consciousness after death, and is able to commune with other souls. This communion, however is purely spiritual in character, and is conditioned upon the disinterested and selfless love of the individuals for each other.'

Tears rolled down my cheeks as Javad asked the rest of the family to leave. I held him tight. I could not stop crying no matter how much he wanted me to be happy. I knew that he was gradually slipping away and I said a quiet prayer as I held him in my arms. He opened his eyes one more time and with a final breath, he was gone, winging his flight into the realm of his Beloved. I closed his eyes and called the children into the room. We gathered around his bed and prayed and cried. My perfect exemplar had passed away peacefully in my arms. He was so much more than words could adequately express. As I sit here years later writing my story, I wish he was here with me. When I look at his picture he seems to say, 'Don't cry. Mano, we will be together one day.' And my reply to him is simply that there is a place in my heart, my mind and my soul that is his alone.

Javad passed away in 1981. The hospital recorded 17 different diseases on his death certificate to mask the injuries he had sustained at the hands of his faceless attackers. There was no point in complaining. Whoever had attacked Javad that night on his way home from the shop in Bushehr had caused him the injuries that led to his death. Of that we were all certain. But it would be a crime that went unpunished. After all, can one be held accountable for assaulting a non-person? I fell asleep that night in widowhood. My body ached with a grief that I could not explain and endless tears rolled down my cheeks.

This wonderful, much loved, loving, caring and kind husband and the father of nine children died just before his marriage of over 40 years was declared null and void by the authorities. The Government wanted to take over his estate, ignorant of the fact that he had nothing. Bahram and Parviz took him in an ambulance to the cemetery. They washed his body and put him in a white silk shroud. Then they put a Bahá'í burial ring on his finger. Since Javad loved rose essence, I sprinkled some on him. His body was laid to rest in Golestan Javid, a Bahá'í cemetery in Shiraz. He was buried next to Mr Vahdat and Mr Mehdizadeh, two Bahá'ís from Shiraz who had been executed some weeks before, and in close proximity to the physical remains of his niece and daughter-in-law. After a further week in Shiraz, the family returned to Bushehr, as successive waves of crisis prepared to batter the shores of our lives.

8

After Javad

Soon after I arrived back in Bushehr I was informed that the marriages of our children had also been declared null and void. I went to the authorities to protest, only to find out that they now had the power to declare my children to be involved in prostitution, a crime punishable by death. Our school-aged children were instructed by their teachers to renounce their faith or not attend school. They enrolled in night classes as a means of continuing their education. After a week, they were asked not to return. My greatest distress was seeing my children and grandchildren being denied an education. They had difficulty in understanding why they could not go to school any more. For Javad and me, the education of our children had been the highest priority. We wanted them all to have opportunities that we hadn't had, and felt that a sound education was the best thing we could give them. Now, we were being denied even the chance to do that.

Our youngest daughter Faranak was 14. She tried to explain to the school principal and teachers that just because she was born in a Bahá'í family didn't automatically give her the right of membership. She said in order to be a Bahá'í she had to investigate the truth, study all the major religions and make a decision when she was at least 15. However, the principal refused to accept her explanation and dismissed her from school. She came home crying, hurt and humiliated. I went to school with her the next day and argued that the lack of education would cause her undue difficulty later in life. They didn't seem to care. I suggested that they should seize the opportunity to teach her about Islam but they didn't seem to care about that either. The principal claimed that my daughter had a very strong character and was already a dedicated Bahá'í and that she had already been persuading other children to investigate the truth for themselves. Any attempts to have Faranak re-enrolled in school were futile. As other Bahá'í families had done, we turned to educated members of the Bahá'í community to help tutor our children at home.

In the early months of the Revolution, Fahimeh, who was studying for a Bachelor of Arts degree in Management at Tehran University, returned home. The campus had become extremely political. Fahimeh had been told to choose which political faction she supported – the Mujahidin, Communists, Hezbollah or the Monarchists. As a Bahá'í, Fahimeh didn't involve herself in party politics, nor did she believe that the partisan political system was the most efficient way of governance. Each group claimed to have the solution and to have a framework for change that Iran had to go through in order to survive. Fahimeh believed in change for the better, but she was not convinced that they knew or had any idea of what sort of change Iran needed. I agreed with Fahimeh, in that I didn't believe that people were anticipating or evaluating the consequences of their actions or the seriousness of their barbaric behaviour. Fahimeh was frightened of some individuals at university who seemed to believe that not belonging to a group was worse than killing another person for not being a member of a group. Some had become overtly hostile, denouncing their best friends, brothers, sisters and close relatives. In the beginning she was barred access to her classes. Then she was refused enrolment for the second semester. In the end she left Tehran University and came home.

All her life Fahimeh had wanted to study and to make her life a success. She used to tell her father that if Fere left, she would stay. If Fere finished one degree, she would finish at least two degrees. But there was no sign of hope, and the radio, television and newspapers did not report anything optimistic. She decided to study from home, starting a two-year diploma course in theology, which she found stimulating and intriguing. When she was studying the qualities of the best leaders in the world, she discovered that the virtues of justice and peace were missing in many of them. In her search for additional information to further her studies, she was informed that in the absence of opportunity for admission of Bahá'í students to tertiary education, the Bahá'í community had decided to establish an open university for them to study by correspondence. There were a number of unemployed lecturers and graduates, not allowed to work, who were enthusiastic to oversee the progress of the Bahá'í Open University.

A young man by the name of Habib came to Bushehr

to run introductory workshops to encourage local youth to participate in the Open University and enrol in the advanced courses. He was a law graduate from Tehran University but was not allowed to practise law because he was a Bahá'í. He had offered himself to the Bahá'í Open University to teach courses including civil law versus religious law and the psychology of all the religions. Whenever Habib was in town, he and Fahimeh had great philosophical discussions on ideas such as world government, international tribunals, international currency and international management systems. He was four years older than Fahimeh and therefore was more mature and positive in his outlook to life and was very instrumental in Fahimeh's development. She was disappointed with the political change that was taking over the country and believed that this change was in fact traumatic and detrimental to the life of individuals and society. She would often complain to Habib. His advice was to be patient. On one occasion I overhead him saying to her, 'A lotus flower shines, radiates and is more lustrous in a muddy pond and the sun rises with full face after the darkness of the night! Just be patient.'

I liked Habib. Whenever he was around, Fahimeh was happy and optimistic and that made me feel happy. It was clear to all of us how fond they were of each other. After a year, they married in a small ceremony. In order to have an income to support his family, Habib learned from Bahram how to fix watches but also spent his spare time in helping the young Bahá'ís and supporting the Open University system. After two years of marriage, Fahimeh and Habib heard that Habib's brother and father had been arrested and sentenced to 10 years imprisonment. He was left with the responsibility of looking after his mother, younger brother, sister-in-law and niece. So Habib and Fahimeh left Bushehr for his hometown in the north of Iran where Habib worked on the family farm with his brother and mother. Habib was a Turkish-speaking Bahá'í from Azerbaijan, but Fahimeh did not speak Turkish, nor were there language classes, so she found it very difficult to communicate. However, their children picked up the language very quickly and after a few months they were interpreting for her. Fahimeh said she was having the experience of living in another country without having to cross the border.

Habib's father was in his early 80s when he was arrested, interrogated and imprisoned. He was asked to renounce his faith. Subsequently he was tortured on a daily basis, and died after two years in prison. Habib said his father never complained about the hardship, severity and ordeal of imprisonment. Habib's brother, who was also in solitary confinement, was not with his father when he died. The ordeal of breaking the news of his father's death to her son made Habib's mother very ill. After serving his 10 years, Habib's brother was released from prison. By then, he had lost his engineering position at the company he worked for and his wife was too old to have another child as she had wished. Their life was nothing but struggle. They lived in absolute poverty.

Our youngest son, Behzad, was called to serve in the military service for two years. He applied for an exemption or to be in a non-combatant position on religious grounds, and was told that in any case combatant positions were reserved for Muslims so were not available to him. The assumption was that if a Muslim soldier were killed in the war, he would go straight to heaven. Because Behzad was considered 'untouchable', he was not allowed to work in a position where he would come in direct contact with the Muslim soldiers. In his initial months of military service, Behzad was made responsible for the acquisition of supplies. On one of his shopping expeditions, a fellow soldier told Behzad that if he were smart, he would pocket the shopping money. Behzad was naturally shocked at this suggestion of dishonesty and asked the soldier why he suggested it. The soldier replied that as Behzad did not have a father, he could use the money to support his family. Behzad explained that he was a Bahá'í and had both a moral obligation and also a civil obligation of trust. The two entered into conversation about Behzad's beliefs. A few days later, Behzad was called in to the office of his commanding officer, who accused him of teaching the Bahá'í Faith and misleading other soldiers. Behzad insisted that this was far from the truth, but the commanding officer chose to believe the other soldier and said that the penalty for such behaviour was execution. However, since there was no other record in his file and he was a soldier of good standing, he was sentenced to four months imprisonment.

Behzad was taken to Tehran and placed in solitary confinement. I contacted some friends and relatives in Tehran, appealing to them to go to visit him in prison, but no one felt able to do so. Some, I am sure, feared for their own safety. In the end, Parviz went to visit Behzad and saw that he could not stand up straight or walk properly. When Parviz touched Behzad's back, Behzad screamed in pain. He later recounted that while he was in prison the guards would regularly whip him to such an extent that the skin had almost peeled off his back. He had deep wounds there. On his next visit, Parviz took some antiseptic cream and painkillers for him. When Behzad was finally released from prison and returned home, it was clear that the torture that he had sustained had traumatized him to an indescribable degree. He told me that his faith had been tested on a daily basis and that it was only his belief that these tests would make him stronger that had enabled him to endure the suffering.

Farideh and Parviz were confident that their decision to return to Bushehr was the right one. They would often say that if God closes a window, He opens a door. Parviz was like a son to us, to such an extent that before Javad passed away he had entrusted the family affairs to him and asked that he look after the family. Parviz felt honoured to be given this responsibility and promised Javad that he would not let him down. He began to help Bahram to run Javad's shop. Farideh by now was very involved with the education of her three children and ran weekly parenting classes as well as fortnightly seminars for young couples on hygiene, family planning and pregnancy.

Among the many limitations placed on the Bahá'í community in Iran as a result of the 1979 Islamic Revolution was the restriction of meetings and gathering together.

No more than three Bahá'ís were allowed to gather in one place at any time. If we wanted to hold our regular community gatherings and Holy Day celebrations, we had to be extremely careful. Shortly after the Revolution, the local administrative institutions of the Bahá'í Faith were banned. As a result, Bahá'ís could no longer elect their representatives. Instead seven people were elected as the '*Yaran*' (assistants) and three individuals in each locality were appointed as '*Khademin*' (servants to the community). A further seven Yaran and three Khademin were appointed as reserves in the event that the first group was arrested or imprisoned. Parviz was one of these Khademin in Bushehr and the authorities often interrogated him about the role he played in the Bahá'í community.

If it were not the imprisonment of one son, it was the personal tragedy in the life of another that continued to test us during those difficult years. In the early 1970s, Bahram, our second son, had fallen in love with his second cousin Fereshteh. She was nearly five years younger than Bahram and her parents did not approve of her marrying so young. In love, both Bahram and Fereshteh wanted to marry, but also wanted to respect the wishes of their parents. Quite apart from their youth, neither Javad nor I believed that family members, including second cousins, should marry each other. We had long hoped that some of our children would travel abroad and meet and marry people of other races and cultures. Despite our reservations, Bahram and Fereshteh never once faltered in their love for and devotion to each other. The bond of love between them was so strong and so amazing to witness that they seemed to be one, united in heart and soul.

We refused to give consent to the marriage, as did Fereshteh's parents. Bahram and Fereshteh never once thought of going against our wishes. They patiently waited and demonstrated through word and deed their commitment to each other and their respect for us as their parents. After five years in which their love never faltered, we finally consented to their marriage. Fere and Abbas travelled all the way from England for the wedding in 1977. Bahram and Fereshteh were so happy that they invited hundreds of people to their wedding, including Bahá'ís, Muslims, and Sufis. Everyone was united in the celebration of this young love. There was love in the air and a great sense of peace and tranquillity filled the most romantic day of that year. As Bahram and Fereshteh left on their honeymoon, they invited Abbas, Fere, Parviz and Farideh to join them in three days time. The six of them holidayed together in the north of Iran.

In their absence, our two families prepared and furnished a two-bedroom unit for the bride and groom. The wedding photos were printed. We decided to have a party in their honour when they returned. Fere, Abbas, Parviz and Farideh returned first and told us that Bahram and Fereshteh would return to Shiraz in a few days after stopping on the way to visit a sick relative who had been unable to travel to the wedding.

As we prepared for their arrival the following day, we received a phone call from the hospital. It was Bahram. His voice was trembling. He said that he had been in a car accident and had rushed the driver of the other car to the hospital for treatment. When they arrived at the hospital, Fereshteh had slipped into a coma and died moments later. I had trouble hearing him, and then felt faint and passed out. When I regained consciousness, I telephoned several hospitals until I found them. We rushed to Bahram's side. When we arrived at the hospital, we found Bahram a broken man. He sat dishevelled, his head in his hands, sobbing uncontrollably. His grief was beyond compare. He cried aloud that he wanted to be dead instead of Fereshteh, that he didn't deserve her, that he didn't want to live without her. There was nothing we could do to ease his suffering or his anguish. Utterly consumed with grief, he stood up and began reciting love poems aloud. In the end we called a nurse to help sedate him and at last were able to take him home.

Fereshteh's funeral was the most moving I had ever attended. It was as crowded as their wedding had been. Wedding pictures adorned the room and we were all reminded that only a month before, Fereshteh had been radiating joy and happiness at her own wedding and here we all were, grieving at her funeral. In the eulogy, Bahram spoke about his love for Fereshteh and how in the years that they had known each other and the few brief weeks they had shared as man and wife, she had come to represent the highest ideal anyone could achieve and how her sense of love and devotion far exceeded anything that he felt he ever deserved. Fereshteh was buried in the Bahá'í cemetery in Shiraz. It was to be only a few years later that Javad would join her there.

My heart was bleeding for my son. I wished I were dead and didn't have to experience this loss. The family was devastated. I was grateful that at least they had had those brief few weeks together, but at the same time I blamed myself for having consented to the marriage. If we had refused to give our consent, they would never have married and would not have been driving back from a honeymoon. Bahram tormented himself with blame. For three days and nights following the funeral, Bahram wept at the cemetery and refused to leave Fereshteh's grave. After several days, we finally coaxed him home, but he would return each day to mourn at the grave of his beloved wife.

Some months later, the Islamic Government ordered the destruction of all Bahá'í cemeteries. The guards who had regularly seen Bahram at Fereshteh's grave asked him to take her body elsewhere so that the grave would not be destroyed. Bahram replied, 'I have been asking her to come with me for a long time but she doesn't.' The guards realized that Bahram was a broken man. Within weeks the entire cemetery was bulldozed.

Bahram's car had been written off in the accident. Not long afterwards he lost his job. Many of his friends were arrested and executed. Then came his father's death. It took Bahram many months to recover to a point where he was able to function as a normal human being. He became determined not to waste what time he had, so he began to assist families that had been displaced as a result of the war with Iraq. Although he was not paid for his service, he found personal satisfaction and great reward in helping those who were less fortunate.

One of those that Bahram helped was a father with five children. Bahram knew this family from his childhood days and brought them back to live in his house. The man's wife had just died and the eldest daughter, Shohreh, was now looking after her father and four younger siblings. Shohreh reminded Bahram of Fereshteh. She was determined and well read. She was easy to talk to, easy to work with and very mature in her outlook on life. She encouraged all the women in our community to take up Bahá'í correspondence courses and she became their tutor. She seemed to have an endless amount of energy and such a positive and happy disposition that all who knew her soon loved her. Bahram, and indeed our whole family, adored her. She brought music and happiness back to Bahram's life. Bahram and Shohreh used to joke that their departed parents met in the next world and brought them together. A few months later, Bahram and Shohreh were married in a very simple and modest ceremony.

It was clear that Shohreh had gained a lot of her perspective from her own mother. She told Farideh that women should have a free choice: to be career women or have the unique role of nurturing and caring for their children. She said mothers were like miners digging for gems, educators polishing the stones, and peace-makers bringing up a new race of people who would be interested in the well-being of humankind. I loved Shohreh dearly. She had everything I had ever dreamed to see in a daughter-in-law. I couldn't stop thanking God for the gift to Bahram and our family.

With the help of some Muslim friends and his father-in-law, Bahram managed to take over his father's shop. The Government approved the transfer of ownership subject to renovation, so he spent all his money and borrowed some more to complete the necessary work. After weeks of tireless work, the renovations were complete and the shop looked magnificent. The future, at last, seemed rosy.

Shohreh's father was concerned about the future of his other four children and had come to realize the significant role his wife had played in their lives. He felt homeless even in his own country and lonely in a crowd. Now with Shohreh married and living her own life, he knew that he must try to find some stability and security for his remaining four children. After much discussion, it was decided that he and the children would leave Iran and flee to Pakistan as refugees. It is hard to forget the day he said goodbye to Shohreh. His eyes were red from tears and as he spoke the words seemed to choke in his throat. He wondered whether he would ever see Shohreh again. With the confidence she always exuded, she calmly replied, 'We will see each other if God is willing.' After anxious days and nights, he finally called from Pakistan to say that he and the children had arrived safely. Some months later, they were accepted as refugees and travelled to Canada where they have now settled. This was to be the fate of thousands of other Iranian Bahá'ís who are spread throughout the world today.

Soon after the departure of Shohreh's father with her brothers and sisters, Javad's shop was confiscated. This was after Bahram had put so much money and effort into renovating the shop under orders from the local authorities, who now simply revoked the licence and confiscated the shop. Bahram tried to engage a lawyer but was told he had no rights in the court and that no lawyer would be brave enough to be an advocate for a Bahá'í. Bahram became very depressed. By this time he and Shohreh had three children of their own with no means to support the family. However, through all this Shohreh never lost sight of the future, nor did she let the troubles of their lives stop her from helping others. She continued with her work educating her children and the women in the community.

At the same time, Parviz and Farideh found themselves without any place to live. All 14 of us ended up living in the same three-bedroom house. The family turned into a production line, cooking, cleaning, sewing and teaching. The children would sleep together in the sitting room, while their parents each had a bedroom. There was no peace and quiet or privacy during the day, but morning prayers, evening studies and discussions were meaningful and brought all the families together. The queues for the bathroom and the toilet were the most inconvenient. Over time, the little ones learnt to respect me as the only older person amongst them and would give up their place for me. After half-a century's experience in negotiating, I was given the task of using the meagre resources of the family to buy food. I never came home from a shopping trip without at least some food, although there were occasions when I had to sell some of our sentimental and cherished belongings to obtain it. Fere's occasional financial help from Australia made it possible for us to survive. Bahram's father-in-law also came to our rescue a few times by sending money from Canada.

Cramped conditions, unemployment and poverty were not our only concerns. The Revolutionary Guards would regularly visit the home of Bahá'ís and confiscate whatever belongings they wished. On the worst occasions they would arrest someone and take him or her for questioning. It was not uncommon for the Revolutionary Guards to lock us all in one room and then go through our belongings, throwing them around the room. They would take books, furniture and pictures, whatever they felt like. There was no use complaining, and eventually we were left with no furniture or anything of any value. The upside, of course, was that because we all slept on the floor without any furniture the rooms were bigger and accommodated us better. On one occasion when we removed a wall to make the room bigger, we found a microphone in the wall cavity. We had no idea when the guards had put it there or why indeed they needed to listen to our conversations. It seemed bad enough not to have privacy with three families living together, but now, knowing that all our conversations had at one point or another been monitored, I wondered why we even bothered with the four walls around us.

9

Visitors from Australia

By 1990 the persecution of the Bahá'ís had to some extent reached a plateau. Although they were still imprisoned and denied opportunities of work and education, the number of Báhá'ís being executed had decreased. In some provinces, Bahá'í children were allowed to return to primary school, but this was entirely at the discretion of the local authorities. The arbitrary nature of the sanctions against the Bahá'í community was difficult to navigate. In one school Bahá'í children would be tolerated while in the neighbouring school they were refused entry. Bahá'ís who had been working one day without difficulty would be dismissed the next. Similarly, when it came to applications for passports to travel outside Iran, some Bahá'ís were given passports while others were denied them. There seemed to be neither rhyme nor reason to this system and this made our lives all the more difficult.

One marked characteristic of the 1979 Iranian Revolution was the number of Iranian professionals who chose to leave the country. Others fled for their lives by virtue of either their political or religious affiliations. The 'brain drain' affected the country greatly; there was a marked shortage of doctors, lawyers, engineers and other professionals. To compound this problem, many of the young male students at university were called to fight in the war with Iraq. Many thousands of these young men were killed, leaving a vacuum in the number of students graduating in professional capacities. As a countermeasure, the Iranian Government began to encourage expatriate Iranian professionals to return to Iran. In most cases they were promised great inducements to return. To many it seemed that the Iranian Government was prepared to overlook political and religious affiliations in order to encourage these expatriates home. Many of the government application forms had removed any question of religion. In cases where it was still asked, it seemed that Bahá'ís were being given less of a difficult time.

This relaxation of procedure encouraged Fere and Abbas, who were now living in Canberra, to make inquiries about returning to Iran for a visit. After many phone calls, it became apparent that Fere could apply and receive a passport to travel to Iran. I was overjoyed when she rang to tell me that she would be coming back to Iran for a visit. She planned to stay for several weeks and said she would be leaving the children with Abbas in Australia. I pleaded with her to bring my grandsons with her so that I could at least see them for the first time. After some discussion, it was decided that Fere and her two sons would travel to Iran in a few weeks time.

After 14 years of being apart, my life became consumed with the thought of seeing Fere again. My child, now a mother of two sons, had become a professional woman abroad. It was almost impossible for me to imagine it.

Fere was due to arrive in Shiraz. We left Bushehr several days before her arrival so that we could prepare for the visit. I could hardly sleep in those last days and counted down the hours and minutes until I would see Fere again. Our taxi arrived at the airport in Shiraz an hour before the flight was due to arrive, but as was quite usual for domestic flights, the plane was delayed. I prayed that they would arrive safely. The plane finally landed, and when from the terminal I saw Fere step from the plane with her ten-year-old and seven-year-old sons, I was so overcome by emotion that I fainted. When I at last came to, we waited patiently for them to collect their luggage and clear customs. After two hours, my nephew went to enquire as to why they had been delayed. It seemed that the airport officials were suspicious why Fere and her children were visiting Iran after so many years. They were also disturbed by the fact that the two young boys could not speak Persian fluently. They also objected to a small keyboard and violin that the children had brought with them, explaining that music was banned in Iran. My nephew, who was an army conscript at the time, explained that he would make sure that the instruments were returned to Australia and that no one touched them in Iran. After much negotiation, the authorities finally allowed them to pass. At long last I was finally able to embrace my child.

There were many tears of joy that day. Fere was in her mid-30s and with her long hair didn't look very much different from the last time I had seen her many years before. I went forward to embrace my grandsons, who promptly told me that they didn't like to be kissed, so I shook their hands instead. Tears of joy and laughter abounded and my grandchildren asked their mother why I was sad. Fere smiled and told them, 'Grandma is happy.'

With tears in her eyes, Fere remembered her father. She said that she had promised to send him a picture when she finished her degree, but because he had died before her graduation, she hadn't bothered going to the ceremony. I assured her that he knew how she felt and that even though he was no longer with us, I was sure that Javad too was rejoicing in this reunion after so many long years. Fere's beautiful honey eyes with her thick black eyelashes reminded me so much of her father. Both her sons looked so much like their uncles. I wondered then what they must have been thinking, arriving in this country that was so foreign to them and to be greeted by family they had never met. I was sure that it was as overwhelming an experience for them as it was for me. Only a mother separated from her child for this length of time could really understand the depth of my feeling.

With the luggage distributed between us, we made our way to the car park. Fere asked where we were going and I told her that we would be staying for a few days in the home of my mother – that same mother who had refused to set foot in my house when Fere was born. Fere was astonished. I explained to her that the Revolution had changed many things, not the least of which was the attitude of my mother. When people were burning the houses of Bahá'ís and yet more Bahá'ís were being executed, my mother could not believe that her fellow Muslims were being so violent to a peace-loving although misguided group. When she heard rumours that Bahá'í women were prostitutes she became very angry and defended my honour, saying that her daughter was a Bahá'í and that she was prepared to put her hand on the Qur'án and swear that I had always been chaste and faithful to my husband. She was ignored and ridiculed. In the midst of these taunts and untruths, she expected the mullah to defend her, but he remained silent. It was only then that she realized her mistake in blindly following his advice to disown her child.

We stayed in Shiraz for a few days with my mother, sister and brother-in-law, who himself – though a devout Muslim – had lost his job for having a Bahá'í sister-in-law. It was a special time for us all, with four generations of the family together at the same time. The whole family were interested in hearing about Fere's experiences abroad, and were all ears when Fere and the children spoke in English. They were amazed that the children could speak English fluently at such a young age, forgetting that in fact English was their mother tongue.

After several days we left the mild, charming spring weather in Shiraz for the much hotter and more humid climate of Bushehr. It was a happy time, and though we had little means, we arranged many occasions for our friends to come and meet Fere and the children and hear about their life and experiences in Australia. For these Bahá'ís in Iran, who had undergone such persecution, there was something very heart-warming in hearing stories of how the Bahá'í communities in other parts of the world were thriving. The stories that Fere told of the Bahá'í activities in Australia strengthened the bond we felt with our fellow Bahá'ís the world over.

Before Fere and the children arrived, we had borrowed some money that would enable us to travel to visit other relatives. We visited Shahpour's Cave near Koziroon, which served as the water reserve for the province. The children were excited to see so much water in a cave. We also travelled to Isfahan, a city with many interesting and historic places, including the Masjid Shah (Royal Mosque), built in the seventeenth century under Abbas the Great. Our visit to Tehran was mainly to see relatives and friends. We also visited the prisons near Tehran where the Bahá'ís were being held but were not permitted to visit the prisoners.

When we returned to Bushehr, friends and relatives began throwing parties in honour of our guests. Golnaz, an old school friend of Fere's, arranged an elaborate dinner party in Fere's honour at her home in one of the more affluent neighbourhoods of Bushehr. Fere arrived wearing a *chador*, and under it her very best clothes. To her amazement, her former school friends arrived in their Mercedes and BMWs, wearing the latest designer European fashions, cleverly concealed under *chadors* until they were inside the house. Golnaz offered Fere a change of clothing, making her feel frumpy and underdressed. Fourteen years before when they had all been at university together sharing the same dormitory, they had all been very religious and pious, praying five times a day and never allowing Fere to prepare food or wash the dishes because they considered her to be 'unclean'. Now, despite alcohol being illegal in post-revolutionary Iran, Fere was offered pre-dinner drinks. The liquor bottles reminded her of the bars of London. When Fere asked for a soft drink, Golnaz thought Fere was kidding, saying that it had taken the rest of them only six months to become westernized. Fere explained that while she might live in a Western country, she had not compromised the principles of her Faith. Golnaz replied that religion was for 'foolish people'. It was then that Fere realized that her devoutly religious friends of years ago had lost their faith and belief, and were as cynical as many other people about the benefits of the Revolution.

During their visit, we went to the unfinished port where the House of the Báb had stood and where Fere had spent many of her childhood years. I showed them the spot where the House had once stood and where the civil engineer of the project, who was not a Bahá'í, had installed a light post with nine globes. The reflection of the globes in the water made it look like a majestic and beautiful star. Fere stood there for a long time, lost in her thoughts and prayers. I was grateful that we could still at least visit the spot where the House of the Báb had once been and where our family had shared so many happy occasions. We also visited a lookout known as 'Galeh Reeshehr' where the Báb had spent time reflecting and meditating. He would walk all day to get to Galeh Reeshehr on the outskirts of Bushehr. When we arrived there, it took us half an hour to climb the hill.

Nevertheless, I was grateful to be with my family on this hallowed ground. As the sun set over the city, we reflected on the life of the Báb and his arduous trials, and prayed that with each day the difficulties of the Bahá'ís in Iran would ease.

The children seemed to adapt well to this foreign country and were soon playing with their cousins and spending time with them. One day my grandson Riaz (Fere's younger son) and his cousin went to town. When they had not returned by nightfall we became very worried about them. Fere wanted to take a taxi and begin looking for them but soon realized that with all the street names having been changed from 14 years before, it would be difficult for her to get any sort of orientation. We sat and waited patiently, while calling friends and relatives to see whether perchance the boys had gone to visit them. Not long into the evening, a taxi pulled up outside the door and the children got out. When Riaz saw his mother he burst into tears and cried that he had had enough of this place and wanted to go back home to Australia. The boys explained that when they had lost their way they had borrowed some money from an old lady to use the telephone, but the two phones they tried were out of order and they had lost the money. They couldn't bring themselves to ask the woman for more money, but later in the evening the old woman had seen them sitting by the side of a road and ordered a taxi to take them home. My heart went out to them – how lost and alone they must have felt in this strange place! We thanked God that night for the generosity of that old woman and for having the boys home safe and sound.

Having my grandsons with me meant that for the first time I was able to see things through their eyes and understand that what for some of us was part of everyday life could be quite a shock for others. On one occasion, just before Fere and the boys were due to return to Australia, we arranged a farewell picnic for them. I decided to cook a Persian delicacy for the occasion known as Kale Pache, which Fere hadn't had for many years. Kale Pache is made by stewing the head of a lamb overnight. This stew is then served with bread. I made this dish with great expectation, hoping that my grandsons would at least try this dish that had been passed down from generation to generation. To my dismay, whatever I tried to offer them, they refused. It was only later that I understood that for them the idea of stewing the head of a lamb was barbaric at best. I vowed then never to make this dish again. Despite these cultural differences there were also bridges, and as our time together drew to a close, I could see that both the boys were making a huge effort to understand my experiences and way of life.

10

Getting Out

Five days before the family was due to leave, Fere took a photocopy of her passport to the passport office as she had been instructed and we prepared for their departure. At the airport in Shiraz I was distraught at the thought that it might be another 14 years before I saw Fere and my grandsons again. But when we arrived at check-in, the customs officer began to inspect their luggage. He took exception to a clock that I had given Fere, which had been her father's, along with a letter that he had written to her before he died. I thought it would be a small memento for her of her time with us and of her father. The customs officer called over the supervising mullah, who determined that the clock was an antique and as such was considered currency and could not be taken out of the country. I thought to myself that the family's intellect was the real currency they were taking out of Iran. The rest of the luggage was checked in without incident and Fere joined the queue where the same mullah was distributing the passports. When she reached the front of the queue she was told that she needed to go to another room to collect her passport. The anxiety on her face was clear when she came back and told us what happened. Her name was then called over the loudspeaker and, together with Parviz, she went to obtain her passport.

Fere and Parviz went to the room indicated, but when they entered it was apparent that the room didn't have any windows and was very dark. Fere looked for a light switch and found none. After some moments, a man appeared from behind a black curtain and told Parviz to wait outside the room and close the door. He sat opposite Fere but didn't make eye contact with her. The official asked a lot of questions, her name, date of birth, profession. After lengthy questioning Fere assumed the interview was over and asked about her passport. The official said that the passport had not been 'classified' and had therefore been sent to Tehran for classification; she could go to the passport office there in a week's time to get it.

Fere was in shock. All she could think of was that they would have to wait a week for their passports. Out of the blue the official asked what religion she was and without thinking, she answered that she was a Bahá'í. The officer began yelling and screaming, demanding that she repeat what she had said. When she again told him that she was a Bahá'í, he flew into a rage. He pushed the table violently towards her and rebuked her for daring to say such an 'insulting' word in front of him. He mumbled 'blasphemous' under his breath and again disappeared behind the black curtain. There was a terrible silence. Tears rolled down Fere's cheeks as it became clear to her that this delay in their departure was for no other reason than the fact that she was a Bahá'í. After what seemed like hours, but in reality was only about ten minutes, the official returned and began asking questions about

Abbas and the children. When Fere explained that they too were Bahá'ís, he was enraged and said that she and her family were lost souls, believers in Satan, and that she had betrayed her country when she became an Australian citizen.

The longer he lectured her and yelled at her, the more Fere thought of her peaceful life in Australia with all its liberties and freedoms. All the things which she had taken for granted up until this moment were suddenly vivid to her. Thousands of miles away from home, alone and vulnerable, she felt more powerless than she had ever felt before. She realized then that she was at the mercy of the Islamic Government and would not be able to leave the country until they gave their permission.

We waited for what seemed like hours. Dana and Riaz were getting increasingly worried about their mother. When it became apparent that Parviz was not going to be allowed in the room with her, I feared the worst – that they might take Fere away or even torture her. After an hour Fere and Parviz returned. I could see that her eyes were red from crying. She hugged the boys but would not let them see her face. She explained to us that she needed to arrange for the luggage to be taken off the aircraft. Both Dana and Riaz asked why they couldn't leave as they had planned. Their innocent eyes looked to us for answers, but we had none. How do you explain to young children that they can't leave the country because of their Faith?

From the airport, we went to the office of the national telephone carrier, where Fere booked a call to Abbas. She explained that their passports had been taken and that they had not been allowed to leave. Abbas was shocked and asked if we had done anything to upset the authorities or if we had broken any laws. Fere was weeping on the phone, explaining that we had done nothing wrong and had obeyed all the laws of the country to the letter. Despite the assurances they had received in Australia from the Iranian Embassy that they could easily travel back and forth, it seemed that this was not to be the case. Abbas advised Fere to follow the procedure that they had been recommended and said that in the meantime he would contact their local Members of Parliament and the Department of Immigration to see if there was anything that could be done from Australia.

That night, we went to stay with a Bahá'í gentleman in Shiraz whose wife and son had been executed for their religious belief. Since their death, he had turned his home into a free guesthouse for visitors to Shiraz. While I stayed with the boys, this gentleman took Fere to see a colonel in the air force who was also a trained lawyer. The colonel listened to Fere's plight, but explained there was nothing he could do to help her. He said that it would have been easier if she had killed someone or was involved in a drug deal. Under those circumstances there might be some chance of assisting her or pleading mitigating circumstances, but as her only 'crime' was that she was a Bahá'í, and that Bahá'ís had no standing under the law in Iran, there was nothing that he could do to assist her.

After five days in Shiraz, Fere, Parviz and I went to the government offices and got our number in the queue of people to be attended to. It took three hours before it was our turn. The mullah who finally spoke to us said that we had two options. The first was that Fere wait for the passport to be classified, which could take any length of time. The second option was that she sign a form recanting her belief in the Bahá'í Faith and declare herself to be a Muslim. The mullah said that as soon as she did this, her passport would be returned to her and she would be free to go.

Fere's eyes met mine and I could sense that she was facing a great test. The mullah gave us the form and told us to wait in the corner of the room. As we sat together, Parviz explained that whether Fere signed the form or not, there was no guarantee that she would be allowed to go. He said that the Government craved every opportunity to use people as an example. If she signed the form, it would be published in the newspaper, she would be interviewed over and over again on television and radio and, as had happened with other people, she would disappear with no trace. Parviz's words had no influence on Fere. She had always known that she could never renounce her faith, and if that meant that she and the children needed to wait in Iran or find another way of leaving, then so be it.

She returned to the mullah and told him that she would not recant her faith. He screamed at her and said he had no time for heretics like her. As we made our way across the room, the mullah called us back and gave Fere an eight-page questionnaire which asked about her parents, brother, sisters, in-laws and so on. With our help,

Fere filled in the questionnaire and took it back to the mullah. At the place for the name of her dead grandparents, Fere had written 'deceased'. The mullah demanded to know which cemetery they were buried in. For Fere, this was the last straw. Before the crowded room of onlookers she burst into tears and asked the mullah to tell her what crime she had committed and why she was being treated in this way. Weeping, she said that other people had come to Iran and returned to Australia without incident and had not experienced this difficulty. The mullah told her that she was lucky to be alive. Parviz and I led Fere, sobbing and in desperation, from the office, not wanting her to find herself in any more precarious a position than she already was.

When we returned to the house, our host saw how despondent Fere was and suggested that we all sit and pray for a resolution to be found. We prayed together. Our host reminded Fere that many women in Bahá'í history had faced hardship and oppression much greater than hers. He spoke of the courage of women such as Tahirih, a poet, wife and mother, who had been the first woman to remove her veil in the company of men and declare the emancipation of women, in 1850. As we sat together, I could see that Fere's desperation was slowly being replaced by a contentment and peace that I had not seen before.

Some hours later Fere again phoned Australia, this time to speak to her work colleagues. As she spoke, she was crying and saying how much she missed them all. This surprised me, as I had always thought that she was lonely in Australia. Fere later explained that in the absence of her family, her friends had become her family and that it was only now that she realized that she missed many of them, just as she had missed us. That evening, after the events of the day and her conversation with her colleagues in Australia, Fere was moved to write a long and heartfelt letter to them. In it she recounted the events that had brought her to this day, how her passport had been taken and that she was not sure if she would ever be able to leave Iran. She explained at length that her only crime was a belief in the Bahá'í Faith. In a country like Australia where individual freedoms and beliefs were respected, she had come to appreciate how treacherous conditions were for her family and friends in Iran. She recalled an Iran that had been modern and progressive, and told them of a country where women were now veiled, their rights non-existent, and where arbitrary justice was handed out which represented neither the letter nor the spirit of the law. Fere wrote about her family and the conditions in which we lived, how many of us were denied work, how our possessions had been confiscated and our children denied an education. She explained that Bahá'ís did not have the right to congregate, and that if they sought permission to gather together the Revolutionary Guards would often disrupt these meetings and literature would be confiscated. Often people would be arrested. In page after page wrought with heartfelt emotion, Fere pleaded for her friends and family to be aware of the plight of the Bahá'ís in Iran and not think that simply because they were a world away it didn't matter. Not knowing whether she would ever return to her life in Australia, Fere remembered them all and asked that they remember her and continue to take up the cause of those people persecuted for their belief in peace and unity.

The following day, Fere asked if she could leave Dana and Riaz with me while she went to Tehran to get the passports. She did not have enough money to pay for all the tickets and, as she did not know where she was going to stay, she felt that it would be easier and safer if she travelled alone. I was worried about the boys because they had been missing their father, and that was bad enough. Now they would be missing both parents. I despaired at my own selfishness in insisting that Fere bring the children with her to Iran.

Fere rang each day that she was away. Abbas and his sisters also rang from Australia to speak with Dana and Riaz. I could hear the boys begging their mother to come back and pleading with their father to come to take them home. When Fere called, the boys always asked to speak with her in English because they were both worried they would forget how to speak the language. After each phone call they seemed to calm down. I was grateful at least that they could hear their parents' reassurances over the phone.

On her visit to Tehran to get her passport she stayed with Parviz's sister, Mrs Karimi. Both Mr and Mrs Karimi had lost their teaching positions because they were Bahá'ís. Their daughter had escaped from Iran to Pakistan and was now also living in Australia. Fere had met her on numerous occasions and was happy that she could at least assure Mrs Karimi at first hand that her daughter was safe, well, and happy and now married with three children of her own. After some days with Mrs Karimi, Fere went to stay with the Layazolee family, who lived much closer to town, thus saving the cost of travel. Mr Layazolee and Parviz were very close. Mr Layazolee had just been released after ten years of imprisonment for being a Bahá'í.

Listening to Mr Layazolee was a source of great strength for Fere. He had endured a great deal of persecution, humiliation and suffering, and yet he was detached and at peace with himself. His daughter had been just a newborn infant when he had been imprisoned, and now, ten years later, he was starting to get to know her for the first time. This family had endured great hardships and trials. While in prison, the guards had played an audiotape of his baby's voice to him. On the tape she was screaming and in the background a woman was crying and begging him to recant his faith so that she and their baby might be spared any further torture and imprisonment. In the midst of this great crisis, he had remained true and steadfast to his Faith. When he was finally released from prison, his wife told him she had never been imprisoned and had never made such a recording. It was yet another means of psychological torture that the authorities used in order to destroy the spirit of their Bahá'í prisoners. One of his punishments while in solitary confinement was administered by a clergyman, who forced him to crawl throughout the cell block so that the other prisoners could laugh and ridicule him. On that occasion, the clergy had asked Mr Layazolee to explain one of the passages from the Bahá'í writings that speak about submitting to God's Will. He did so and was then given 72 lashes for being outspoken, even though he had done so at the clergyman's bidding.

Mrs Layazolee told Fere how time and again she would travel for several hours with her two young children to see her husband, only to have the guards trick her by saying that her husband had been moved to another prison, or that they had 'changed their minds' about allowing her to visit. Living as a single mother with two young children, no income, no support, and no entitlements, Mrs Layazolee would say that her only strength came from visiting her husband, yet even then they were often denied even that simple pleasure. For Fere, it was a great source of encouragement to hear the stories of such strong and steadfast people. She resolved that she too would show forbearance and patience in the face of her own difficulties, and gain strength from the experiences of her hosts.

After several days it was time for Fere and Parviz to travel to the passport office and go through the necessary procedure to retrieve the passports. They waited patiently at the bus stop, the first bus being for women only and the following two being only for men. The fourth bus was one for mixed gender and was very full. Fere got on at the back of the bus where the women were seated and hoped that Parviz had found room at the front of the bus. As the bus began to pull away from the stop, Fere realized that

Parviz had not boarded and began calling for the driver to stop. Fere had no money, did not know where she was going and felt increasingly uncomfortable because the women were laughing at her and the men were eyeing her with interest. The bus driver, amused with this spectacle, stopped the bus and asked some of the men to wait for the next bus so that there would be room for Parviz. Because the men and women were separated, Fere could not speak with Parviz for the entire journey. At each stop she stood and looked to see if Parviz was getting off the bus or not. The woman sitting next to her was intrigued by this routine, so Fere explained her difficulty. To her surprise, it seemed that this woman sympathized with her plight. Using Fere's example she began to speak of Iran's lack of development and oppression of minorities. She then told Fere that the bus was approaching the interchange and that she would need to change buses there. For Fere, it was a valuable lesson in realizing that her fellow Iranians were not all callous, that many were sympathetic to her situation and predicament. When Fere went to change buses, the woman warned her to be wary, for the city had many 'sharks'.

When Parviz and Fere at last found their way to the offices of the Islamic authorities and reached the reception desk, they were told that the office would only see women on Tuesdays and Thursdays. Because she had arrived on a Saturday, the office could not help her. Fere was furious. After her ordeal on the bus in the morning, she refused to return the same way. She and Parviz took a taxi home. The following Tuesday, Fere and Parviz repeated the same journey. When they arrived this time, they were told that the place numbers had been given out at 4 a.m. and that they would not be seeing any more people that day. On Thursday, they repeated the journey yet again and were there early enough to be given number 29 in the queue. Although Parviz had accompanied her, Fere felt insecure and vulnerable; she sensed that there was to be more trouble for them in the process of retrieving her passport. At 8:30 a.m. the clerk announced that the mullah was coming. Those people gathered in the waiting room began reciting a verse from the Qu'rán in praise of Prophet Muhammad. When the mullah finally arrived, the entire group rose to their feet, invoked God in praise and then sat down again. The mullah was dressed in a long robe. Through other women in the room, Fere discovered that he was the son of one of Iran's leading clerics.

After hours of waiting, Fere went in search of amenities and was amazed to be told that there were no public facilities in the building. She went outside in search of a public toilet and finally had to resort to knocking at the door of a private house to ask if she could use their facilities. After thanking the kind strangers, Fere made her way back to the offices and on her way encountered an Englishman who was looking for the passport office. This man was somewhat relieved to discover that Fere could speak English. After she had given him directions, they engaged in a lengthy conversation during which time Fere explained to him her own predicament. He was astonished at her story and promised that he would make sure that those outside Iran knew of her plight and the plight of so many other Bahá'ís.

Returning to the waiting room, Fere took her place among the other women and sat down. As women are wont to do, they began to converse and through various stories discovered that the offices had originally belong to a very prominent family who had left Iran in fear of persecution. Fere explained to them that she wanted to return to Australia but that her passport had been taken and she was trying to retrieve it. The women waiting with her seemed genuinely concerned for her well-being and appeared somewhat surprised that someone would be kept in Iran against their wishes.

After hours of waiting, a man appeared at the door dressed in a military uniform and called out Fere's surname. She stood up and the man ordered her to follow him. As she walked away from the women, she heard their whispers of 'May God be with you' and 'I pray for you'. He pointed to a room with the newspaper that he was holding, asked Fere to wait and closed the door behind her.

Fere would later tell us that the room had neither a table nor a chair and the window had been blacked out so that there was no natural light at all. Fere failed to find a light switch. Realizing that the light switch must be outside, Fere tried to open the door and found that it was locked from the outside. She called for one of the officers to turn on the light, but he ignored her. She asked one of the other women to turn the light on, but no one dared. At last one brave woman went and spoke to the officer, asking if he might just turn the light on for Fere. He screamed at her, saying that Fere could speak for herself and did not need anyone to be an advocate on her behalf. It finally occurred to Fere that this was yet another way in which the authorities were trying to unsettle her. She relented and accepted that she would wait in darkness. She began pacing the room, saying prayers she had memorized, reciting poetry she knew by heart, asking herself questions to keep her mind alert and active. She wondered what prisoners like Mr Layazolee could have done for ten years, locked in a small room. Finally, after what seemed like an eternity, she sat by the door and wept. She wept for her husband and children, for her friends and family, for her predicament, for all the things in Australia she missed, for the freedom she had taken for granted. And, as was inevitable, she began wondering what would happen if they didn't let her go. She concluded that Abbas would move on with his life, he might marry again and sell their house. Immediately her thoughts went to Dana and Riaz, the two sons she had brought back to Iran with her. Suddenly she realized that she was responsible for bringing the children to Iran and subjecting them to these difficult conditions and the prospect of never being able to leave. Fere would later tell me that all her life she had wished she was someone else. When she was a girl going to school, she wished she were a boy; when she went to university in England, she wished she were English. She had spent many years always wishing to be something else, until she became a mother. It was in this role as mother and educator of her own children that she had found a satisfaction she had not known before. All her career ambitions took second place to her role as a mother, but there in a dark room in a government office Fere somehow let go of Dana and Riaz and resigned herself to whatever was to happen to her. She felt sure that if she were unable to leave Iran, Abbas would come and take the boys home, or the family would find some way of sending them out of Iran. She felt sure that the same God who had blessed her with children would Himself look after them, and she felt an aura of peace and contentment envelop her. For years she had recited the prayer:

> O God! Refresh and gladden my spirit, purify my heart, illumine my powers. I lay all my affairs in Thy hand. Thou art my guide and my refuge. I will no longer be sorrowful and grieved. I will be a happy and joyful being. O God! I will no longer be full of anxiety nor will I let trouble harass me. I will not dwell on the unpleasant things of life. Thou art more friend to me than I am to myself. I dedicate myself to Thee, O Lord.

At last she felt that her spirit was both refreshed and gladdened. She stood in that darkened room, resolving that she would not let these difficulties dampen her resolve and her spirit. As she contemplated this, she heard the officer calling for number 39. Knowing that she was number 29, she feared that they had forgotten her. She banged on the door, asking for someone to respond. Finally an officer opened the door. Fere told him that she heard them calling number 39, but that she was number 29, and thought they might be calling for her. The officer replied, 'You have a file here. You do not need a number,' and with that he ushered her back to the now empty waiting room. After speaking on the phone briefly, he turned to Fere and informed her that her file was not ready and that she needed to come back the following week.

Fere could not believe what she was hearing. She had suffered for two days to be there before dawn in order to receive a number in the queue, only to be told that she didn't need a number. She had spent hours in a dark room, only to be dismissed and told to come back the following week. Fere pointed to the Arabic inscription above the officer's head and asked him if he knew what it meant. Indignantly he replied that it meant 'Islam Means Peace and Justice'. With that, Fere told the officer that she had not received peace or justice, but had suffered tyranny, at the hands of the public officials. She complained to him that her family had been fragmented on the whim of these officers, who had chosen to put her through such difficulty in order to retrieve her own passport – her family in the south, herself alone in the north, her husband in Australia. She asked the officer to look at how she had been treated and to decide for himself whether this was justice or not. She questioned his knowledge of Islam and warned him of the consequences of treating people so unjustly. I was grateful that it was late in the day and the officer was tired and merely told Fere to leave, for her criticism of him and allegations that he was not being a 'good Muslim' would certainly have been enough to have her severely punished.

Fere decided to spend the week with her children rather than alone in Tehran, and so returned to Bushehr where we were overjoyed to see her safe and well. In the following week of waiting, Fere knew that people were following her in the streets. For her own safety and that of the family she slept in a different place each night. She did not want her family and friends subjected to interrogation as to her whereabouts and felt that it was best never to stay in one place for very long. After the week had gone by, Fere decided to make inquiries in Shiraz with regard to the passports and took Dana and Riaz with her. The night before they were due to go to the passport office, Abbas called and said that a fax had been sent from Australia and that Fere should specifically inquire as to the outcome of the fax.

We arrived at the office very early and were told to wait. Both Fere and I felt uncomfortable with the clerk behind the desk constantly looking at us. He had the odd habit of rubbing his fingers together. Finally Fere went back to the desk and asked if they had received a fax from Australia. He said he had received it but could not read it and that the translator who worked for them was not there this week and that we would have to return the following week. After much discussion back and forth, the clerk reluctantly gave Fere an appointment.

As we left the office, disappointed yet again by the futility of our attempts, I noticed a ragged old man following us at some distance. As we walked through the lobby and out into the street he caught up with us. We were both suspicious of his motives, so Fere turned around and asked who he was and what he wanted. Sheepishly the man turned away, mumbling under his breath, but after a moment he turned back and said that Fere sounded like a foreigner, and could he ask her something. Naturally, Fere was somewhat apprehensive and told the man she would answer him depending on the question he wanted to ask her. The old man assured Fere that it was not a personal question and proceeded to ask whether her 'problem' with the authorities had been resolved. Fere responded that it hadn't been, in reply to which the old man asked whether the clerk at the counter had been rubbing his fingers together. Fere recalled the annoying habit she had noticed upstairs and told the old man that she had indeed noticed this, what did it mean? The old man explained that money bought many things in the stores in Iran but that it also bought an easy passage through the maze of government bureaucracy. The clerk rubbing his fingers together was his signal that he was open to receive money in exchange for assisting them with their passports. Fere was astounded by what the old man was telling her. She flatly refused to pay any sort of bribe for a right to which she was entitled. Later, I told her that I was proud of her and would support whatever decisions she made and make whatever sacrifices were necessary for her safety. Although no closer to getting her passport back, at least now we had a better understanding of how the system worked.

As she had been instructed to do, Fere and Parviz went to Tehran the following week. Simply travelling together posed some risk to both of them, as by law a woman was not permitted to travel with anyone other than her father, brother or husband. The authorities had been known to randomly ask people to prove their relationship to each other. Stories abounded of young people forced to marry because they had been seen together in public. A friend of ours also recounted how on one occasion she had almost been forced to marry her own brother, as neither had any identification with them that proved their relationship as brother and sister. Although Fere was married, she did not have a marriage certificate that showed her legal marriage to Abbas. As for Parviz, his marriage had been declared void, as had the marriages of many other Bahá'ís. But we all agreed that it would be impossible for Fere to travel by herself, because women travelling alone were often subject to harassment. Both Fere and Parviz were fortunate that the authorities did not question them.

Their trip to Tehran was as eventful as their other journeys there had been. En route, guards who were looking for illegal immigrants from Afghanistan, who they thought were stowing away, stopped their bus. During the long journey, the bus driver was playing music on the radio. Because the Islamic Government had banned music, the guards ripped the radio from the console and threw it out onto the road. The driver was incensed and began throwing everything he could out of the bus in protest. Seeing the rising anger of the driver, the guards ordered the bus on its way. Some time later, the second driver awoke from his nap and inquired as to what had happened to his radio. The two drivers then began an altercation. Fere and the other passengers became increasingly nervous while the two drivers began fighting among themselves. After a brief stop, which served to calm the situation, the drivers reached some understanding as to what had happened to the radio. Soon they were all on their way again.

On arriving in Tehran, Fere and Parviz went to stay with some friends and began the process of tracking down the passports. In the first instance, Fere went to the Australian Embassy, hopeful that they might be able to assist her because she was an Australian citizen. The Embassy officials were sympathetic to her situation, but explained that since she was travelling on an Iranian passport they could be of no service to her because Fere was in Iran and not in Australia. They explained that the Australian passport guaranteed the citizen consular assistance in every country except the country of their birth and original nationality. Fere doubted that this statement was true because firstly she did not know the law, and secondly Abbas had called and said that he had been promised by the Australian authorities that they would do everything they could to get Fere and her children out of Iran.

After further inquiries at various offices, Fere and Parviz again went to the passport office. On this occasion the clerk simply threw her passport in her face and told her to leave Iran immediately. When Fere examined the passport against the photocopy she had kept, there was no marking or any indication that it had been 'classified', as the authorities had claimed. It appeared to be simply a case of causing as much distress to a Bahá'í family as they possibly could. Both Fere and Parviz were astonished. After the difficulty and great lengths they had gone to, on this occasion retrieving the passports had been simple! Soon they were returning to Bushehr so that Fere and the boys could prepare to leave.

With the help of friends and relatives, Fere booked three seats for herself and the children for a flight leaving from Shiraz. Although Iranians generally arrive *en masse* to greet or bid farewell to visitors, when it came time for Fere and the children to return, no one made a fuss about seeing them off. Given the difficulties they had experienced before, there didn't seem to be much of a guarantee that she would leave this time anyway.

At last the day arrived; we again borrowed some money to enable us to travel to the airport in Shiraz. Their flight was due to depart at 6:30 a.m. and we arrived in plenty of time for the flight, well before dawn. When Fere went to check in, she saw that the same mullah who had confiscated their passports was again overseeing operations at the airport. With a sense of foreboding, Fere went forward, only to be told that there had been a delay and that she should come back in a few hours time. We went home again, returning two hours later only to be told that this time there was engine trouble. The officers at the airport again told us to go home and come back in a few hours. This routine went on and on until well into the evening. Finally, when we returned at 8:30 that evening, Fere was told that she had missed her plane. We were all dumbfounded, and Fere simply burst into tears. It was agonizing for me to see her and the children treated in this manner. Although I knew there was nothing that I could do to remedy the situation, I wished that there were. After a few minutes, however, Fere regained her composure. She asked me and the rest of the family to go home and said that she and the children would merely wait until the next flight, whenever that happened to be. She told me that in the face of all of this cruelty and bad treatment, she would retain her dignity and composure and would not allow the authorities the satisfaction of seeing her distraught.

I embraced my daughter for what I was sure would be the final time and told her to go home to Australia and never come back. I could not dream of her having to go through such difficulties again. I knew, as I left her and the children there at the airport, that a power and strength greater than mine would be watching over them. Although Fere had told me to go home, I wasn't able to do so. I waited outside the airport, praying that they would be able to leave safely. After an hour and a half I saw a plane leave, and prayed that Fere and the children were safely aboard. Fere would later tell us that as we left, the mullah, no longer intent on creating any more chaos for Fere, simply stamped the passports and pointed for them to wait in the lounge. I would hear later from my mother and sister that Fere had called them at 11 p.m. to say that she had not waited very long and was indeed on board the plane I had hoped she was. Thus ended Fere's journey home and the sojourn of my visitors from Australia.

11

Faranak's Story

Our youngest child Faranak escaped from Iran in 1995 and arrived in Australia as a refugee in December that same year. She was the only one of my children who wanted to leave Iran after the Revolution, but I refused to let her go until she was at least 18 years old and able to make the decision herself. But when she turned 18 it wasn't possible for her to leave, and she patiently waited for an opportunity to present itself. Faranak had been only five years old when Fere had left Iran for England, and she had always wanted to follow in her older sister's footsteps.

When Faranak was 13, the principal of her school told her she could not continue to attend school unless she publicly declared at the school assembly that she was a Muslim. Faranak replied that she was too young to make such a serious decision, even though the principal insisted that Muslim children made up their minds when they were only nine years old. Unwilling to recant her faith, Faranak stopped going to school for a week, but she missed her friends terribly. When she did return to school, every day would begin with the same interrogation and insults. A year passed, with Faranak consistently subjected to questioning from the principal and teachers for no other reason than the religion in which she had been raised. At the end of that year she was given an ultimatum – she had one more week to make a decision about her future. By the end of that week, Faranak realized that she did not have the energy to fight with the school any longer. She was disappointed, belittled and demoralized and felt completely betrayed by the education system. On the one hand she was told by her parents, her Bahá'í teachers and other adults in the community that the Bahá'í Faith said children should be regarded as 'a mine rich in gems of inestimable value' and that these gems could be polished through education. On the other hand, she had lost her right to be educated and was denied access to a process which was meant to bring out her best.

Faranak enrolled in a night class at a further education institute. She was instantly popular among her classmates; in addition to being naturally bright, she was an attractive young girl. She was certainly the teacher's favourite until it was discovered that she had been born into a Bahá'í family. She had to face the same consequences and suffer the same fate as she had endured at school. With this avenue of further education denied her, Faranak enrolled in sewing classes, but again after a week she was asked to leave. The teacher explained that some of the students had complained about having 'untouchables' in the class and having to share equipment with her.

Faranak felt frustrated, isolated and ostracized. She didn't have a job. She didn't have a place in school. She was downhearted and sorrowful. She felt that the only future she would have was as a wife and mother, but even then, a young Muslim man would never consider marrying a Bahá'í, and almost all of her male Bahá'í peers had escaped from Iran and settled in other countries as refugees. Faranak certainly didn't have the same opportunities as her older sisters. With the continued persecution of the Bahá'í community, their social infrastructure had also been demolished. The Bahá'ís could no longer gather together for the conferences or summer schools that had afforded young people an opportunity to meet one another. Government authorities had confiscated the Bahá'í Centre that used to be the hub of such activity, so this left little opportunity for Faranak and other young Bahá'ís of her age.

It became clear later on, through investigations by the United Nations and their agencies, that the Government of Iran had instituted policies aimed at eradicating the Iranian Bahá'í community. The expulsion of Bahá'í children from schools and higher education, the termination of employment contracts for Bahá'ís, the confiscation of their property, the denial of their access to pensions, social security or health care were all part of a systematic plan of persecution.

Faranak was living through the consequences of these policies. She gave up the idea of education and instead volunteered her services to the Bahá'í community as a kindergarten teacher for Bahá'í children. This, however, motivated her to educate herself at home. After two years of hard work, she sat for and passed her Year 11 exams. But although she was motivated to continue, this avenue was again closed when the Government insisted that home-educated students declare their religion before completing any further exams.

At last, Faranak decided that she wanted to leave Iran to seek her fortune elsewhere. She was unable to study, had no possibility of employment and had no income. Fere had been supporting her financially up to that point. Faranak now applied time after time for a passport, but each time her application was rejected and her application fee lost. When she objected to what was happening, she was told by an official that she was lucky to be still alive.

On one occasion I decided to accompany her to the passport office, as I felt that having her mother with her might afford her some better consideration. The man at the counter tried to persuade me to stop her from applying and leaving Iran. He criticized the Western world, referring to its lack of religion, spirituality and belief in God. He said he knew about the corruption of the West, the extremes of sexual freedom, alcohol, drugs, feminism, gay movements and communism. He said that if I really loved my daughter and cared about her I would not throw her to the lions. He looked into my eyes and said, 'Mrs Saatchi, there is a jungle out there. Look after your lamb.' In response I declared that one could consider the whole world to be corrupt if one looked hard enough, and to his amazement I claimed that our own backyard was the worst. He naturally disagreed. However, I knew, and he knew, that in reality Iran was bad enough to make Faranak run away. Once again I voiced my opinion, saying that she needed to be strong and virtuous no matter where she was on this planet. I added that I had not given birth to a willow tree that sways with the wind, I had given birth to a child who was as strong as a palm tree. He acknowledged that if Faranak was as strong in her convictions as I claimed, I must have done a good job in raising her. I thought, 'Finally we must be getting through to him,' and I appealed to his fair judgement to allow Faranak a chance to leave Iran. But despite our pleas and lengthy discussions, her application was rejected yet again.

Life for Faranak had become unbearable. She had no hope for the future – even her young kindergarten students noticed the sorrow in her eyes. From her vantage point, her life, career, education and personal and professional development all seemed destined to amount to nothing. She told me several times about how miserable she felt, and how she felt that she was a burden to me financially because she was not able to support herself or contribute to our expenses. She told me that if it had not been for me, she would have left Iran long ago. I now believe that it was at that time that she began to make plans to leave. I noticed her hurried and whispered conversations with Fere and others on the phone. When she began to start packing a small bag, I assumed that she was heading north to visit her sister Fahimeh, but a few days before she left, Faranak told me that she was not going to visit Fahimeh but had made arrangements to escape Iran through Pakistan. She asked me to please accept her decision and assured me that she had found some reliable people to travel with. I was sick with worry, and apprehensive about the dangers she would face. She assured me that just as Fere had left all those years before, she too would leave and find her way to Australia and that I had no reason to worry. She assured me that Fere would help her all she could and would support and look after her once she arrived in Australia. I travelled with Faranak to Tehran, wanting to accompany her on as much of the journey as I could. As we flew high above the clouds, both our thoughts went to the passport office staff who thought that they had effectively 'clipped her wings' in denying her a passport. She said she would send them a postcard from Australia. Faranak had a winning smile on her lips. Her starry eyes were like a mirror in which I could see her dreams and the vision of Australia. I was aware of her excitement and prayed for her safety.

A man in his sixties had kindly agreed to have Faranak accompany him and his wife on this trip. The Australian Government had accepted his application for migration on the grounds of family reunion and had offered him an entry visa valid for three months, long enough to organize himself and his family and get ready for the trip. Like many Bahá'ís, he was suffering from injustice. He had been denied the right to his superannuation entitlements and pension and had even been forced to repay salaries he had earned while in a government position. His passport had been confiscated and therefore his only option, like Faranak, was to escape from Iran and hope that once in Pakistan he would be able to travel to Australia and be reunited with his family.

When we arrived in Tehran I rang the number they

had provided, and was told I had the wrong number. I became anxious and thought Faranak was wrong to have blindly trusted a stranger. I said to her that we were lucky we hadn't paid any money in advance, because it appeared that something was wrong with the arrangements. Faranak called two hours later and they recognized her voice and acknowledged who they were. They apologized for the earlier mix-up but were so afraid that their plans might be detected that they were not speaking to anyone whose voice they did not recognize. Faranak made arrangements to meet them at the bus depot at five o'clock the following morning.

In the silence of those hours before dawn, I prayed for the safety of my child as she embarked on this arduous trip. My mind was full with visualizations of all the dangers she might face. I conversed with my Creator. I knew in my heart that Faranak had been given to me as a gift and that I had looked after her to the best of my ability and that God could take her away whenever He willed. I knew she was old enough to leave her homeland and me and fulfil her dreams. I had raised her to always follow her heart's desire and strive to be the best she could be. I knew it was impossible for her to realize that goal in a country where every opportunity was denied her. I had raised Faranak to know that more important than a worldly education was a spiritual education, and that as long as she was true to her spiritual self she would find both success and happiness.

It had, however, seemed easier for me to part from my other children than from Faranak. The thought of her leaving was causing me endless pain. I recalled the conversation I had had with Fere when she and her children had at last managed to leave Iran after their visit. Just as I knew then, I knew now that Faranak would not be coming back and that this might well be the last time I saw her. When the time came to leave for the bus depot, Fahimeh and her husband and children joined us. They too realized that this might well be the last time they saw Faranak.

At the airport, she looked for a man described as tall and in his late sixties. He was said to have plenty of hair, be immaculately shaved with the smell of after-shave, wearing a suit and a tie and walking with his wife, nearly 20 years junior to him. The bus depot was crowded with older people. We were a nation of older people now, with so many of the younger generation either lost in the battlefields or lost to other countries. All of a sudden Faranak ran and cried out, ‘Baba, Baba!’ I thought she was hallucinating – this was what she called her father. I had not heard her say that word for a long time, maybe over a decade; Javad had died when Faranak was only nine years old.

An older man stopped and turned towards us. He introduced himself and his wife briefly and indicated that they had only a short time to catch the bus for Zahedan, a town near the border of Pakistan. He was pleased that Faranak had listened to him and did not have much luggage with her. He advised her not to speak Persian during the journey, as they hoped to disguise themselves as Kurds and pass over the border without drawing attention to themselves.

The road from Bushehr to Shiraz, showing the mountain ranges to be crossed

Above: Anti-Bahá'í graffiti: 'Jihad against the ungodly'

بسمه تعالی

(فرم د)

شماره داوطلب

اینجانب   دارای شماره شناسنامه

متولد   داوطلب امتحان گزینش دانشجو در سال تحصیلی ۷۲-۱۳۷۱ پرونده‌ام

از لحاظ عدم انتخاب دین ناقص می‌باشد، با علامت (×) دین خود را مشخص و کارت

ورود به جلسه خود را دریافت نمودم .

۱ - ☐ اسلام

۲ - ☐ مسیحی

۳ - ☐ کلیمی

۴ - ☐ زرتشتی

محل امضاء

University entry form, 1992–93. Bahá'ís are denied entry through the statement: 'As I do not belong to one of the following religions, I am not entitled to an entry form or registration form.' The form shows four possible boxes: Muslim, Christian, Jewish and Zoroastrian

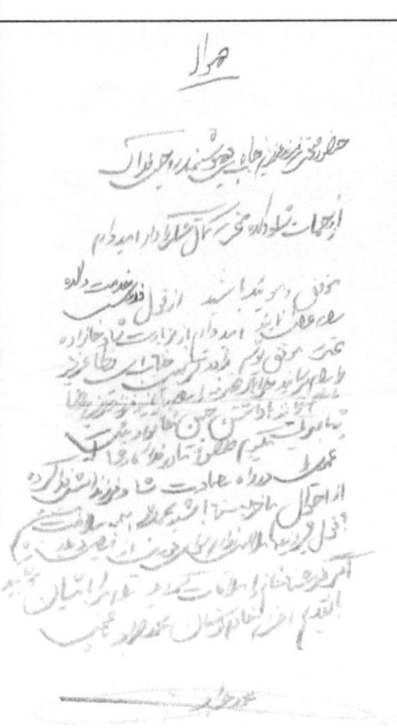

Last letter from Javad Saatchi to his son-in-law Abbas Hooshmand

The Bahá'í cemetery in Shiraz following its destruction by the Islamic authorities in the 1980s. Javad Saatchi, Manijeh's husband, and her daughter-in-law Fereshteh were buried here

Manijeh in Australia, 2012

There wasn't enough time for me to get to know this older couple. All I could do was trust Faranak to their care and to God's. I kept wondering whether they could be trusted, whether they indeed knew what they were doing and whether their advice was sound. I had to reassure myself that there was a plan of God, which was much bigger and better than mine. We need to take steps to confirm our faith, and for me, this was one of those steps.

I gave Faranak some money to buy clothing in Zahedan typical of the kind worn by the nomads of that region. I noticed that the older man was taking photographs as a reminder of this part of their journey and I asked Faranak to send me a photo of her dressed in the clothes of the nomads. We said our farewells and I left my youngest child to the protection of God. I returned to Tehran, but my heart was travelling with my daughter as she made her way to the border with Pakistan. My mind was so preoccupied in the following days that I barely recall whom I spoke to or what I said.

When Faranak was six years old, she had asked me to tell her which was the best house that she had lived in. After thinking for a while, I told her that her best home had been my womb. She wondered why, and I explained that while she was a part of me she had everything she needed: warmth, nutrition, shelter, love and protection. When she was born I felt empty, but that emptiness was replaced with inexplicable joy as I looked down at the child lying next to me. Now I felt empty once more and Faranak was gone. Immersed in my own sad thoughts, with my head resting heavy on my hand, I cried aloud until there were no more tears. Then I sat quietly for a few minutes and meditated. A gentle breeze wafted over my head and a thought pushed its way into my mind. A voice in my head said, 'I thought I said your lives should never be sad, dull, dreary or boring. The way you are carrying on, one would think there is a spiritual law to be in mourning.'

'The opposite is true,' I answered. 'We should be joyful and inspiring so that we become like a magnet attracting others.'

With this conversation playing out in my head, I heard the phone ring. It was Faranak. She was laughing and happy and explained that they were safely in Pakistan and out of danger. She said, 'Mum, you should have come with me.' Then she went on to explain how the escape to Pakistan had been for them. Just before she ran out of money for the phone she said, 'Mum. You know that I can't come back and I might never see you again. You have to try to come out. Please forgive me, Mum. I didn't do this to hurt you. I did this because I had no other choice.'

I loved that phone call. I had just managed to energize my soul with thought-provoking ideas when she had called. I admired her courage and felt proud of her. I wished I were there with her. Two weeks later I received a letter from her telling me her escape story. I sent her some of her old clothes with some sun-dried fruits. She rang regularly from Pakistan to let me know that she was in touch with Fere in Australia. Four months later she called to say that the United Nations had accepted her as a displaced person and that her file had been transferred to the Australian Embassy in Karachi. A month after that, she said her application for a visa for Australia under the 'women at risk programme' had been approved and that she was hoping to be reunited with Fere after passing the final few medical examinations.

I waited anxiously for each report of her progress along this path to freedom. My greatest joy came five weeks later when Faranak rang from Australia saying that she was with Fere in Canberra. Some weeks later, she sent me a copy of an article that had appeared in a newspaper in Australia describing her escape from Iran and the persecution of the Bahá'ís in that country. Accompanying the article was a picture of Fere and Faranak standing side by side. My heart rejoiced when I saw the two sisters together at long last. What does a mother want but the happiness of her children? My task was complete. There was nothing else I wanted from God. I praised the Lord for giving me peace of mind. Every journey starts with one step. She had taken her first step and made it. I never saw her so courageous. I didn't know my own child.

12

Going Home

I missed Faranak a great deal. The only child out of nine who was still at home, because she was not yet married, Faranak and I had a special bond, especially after her father had died. Whenever she called from Australia I could not speak at first and had to cry and get the anguish of our separation out of my system. She would say, 'Mum, please don't cry. You must believe in positive action. Do something about it.'

It was clear that Faranak wanted me to leave Iran and join her and Fere in Australia. She would mention this every time she rang. It was harder for me to think of leaving than it had been for her. Faranak was at the beginning of her life with all the possibilities ahead of her; I, on the other hand, was at the other end of the spectrum. I had lived my entire life in Iran. The thought of leaving was unimaginable. I could not bring myself to leave the cradle of the Faith, or for that matter to leave Javad behind. Even though the government authorities had destroyed the cemetery where Javad was buried, still I had a connection with him there that I was sure I would lose if I left. Of course, there were the other children, now grown men and women, and all my grandchildren, who gave me much hope for the future. Besides, I told Faranak, I was too old to learn English.

Although I had not reached any decision to leave, I decided that there would be no harm in at least applying for a passport. Sure as I was that they would reject my application, I thought this would be the final confirmation that I was supposed to stay in Iran. In the meantime, my own health began to deteriorate and my heart began to give me increasing problems. I had first had a heart attack when Fere had left Iran with her children. I had collapsed outside the airport and a passer-by had called for an ambulance. I was in hospital for a week on that occasion and even before that, when Javad had passed away, I had begun taking medication for my heart condition. When Faranak left, the heart condition became worse; my doctor informed me that I was in urgent need of bypass surgery and admitted me to hospital, but there I was told that because I did not have any health insurance they could not perform the operation. Bahram contacted Fere and she agreed to cover the costs. She found someone who had money in Iran but was unable to take it out of the country, and they gave us the money after she transferred the equivalent amount into their Australian bank account.

While I waited in hospital for my turn to come, a nurse told me that a heart surgeon who worked at that hospital had applied for a scholarship to work in the United States and that the condition of the scholarship was that he utilize a new technique in bypass surgery. The nurse asked me that since I had no money and no insurance, would I be willing to be the guinea pig for this new procedure. She explained that, if successful, it would not only assist my heart condition but it would also allow this doctor to work abroad. My family was naturally apprehensive. They were very protective of me and didn't want me to be the subject of an experimental procedure. After more tests were carried out, Parviz informed me that one of the doctors had signed the necessary forms required by the insurance company and therefore the company would cover part of the cost of the operation. I thought to myself that he must be a very powerful and important doctor to have such sway with the insurance companies. When I asked Parviz if I still needed to have the experimental procedure, he explained that if I did, the cost would be free but if I didn't I would still need to pay for part of the operation.

After consulting with my family, I agreed to undergo the experimental procedure and signed the necessary forms. At that moment I thought how much easier if would be if I died, so that my family would not need to be burdened with my care. I resolved that if my time came, I would not fight it. After all, in the next world I would be reunited with Javad. I figured that if God had further plans for me, the operation would be a success, and if not, at least I was furthering the cause of medical science. The nurse informed me that the operation would take several hours. After saying good-bye to my family I was taken to the operating room and put under a general anaesthetic.

The day after the operation I heard a gentle voice calling my name. It was so loving that I felt sure it was Javad. Half opening my eyes, I looked up and saw a man sitting on my bed. I felt I knew him. Our eyes met and I was sure

I was dreaming. I thought to myself that it could not possibly be true. He held my hand in his and softly called my name, Fatimih. It had been over 50 years since anyone had called me Fatimih. When I had become a Bahá'í as a young teenager I had changed my name to Manijeh, and now this man was calling me Fatimih, the name I had been given at birth and had used as a child. He asked me how I was feeling and I responded that I was not really feeling all that well. He asked if I could tell him who he was. I said that he was probably a doctor but there was something about him that struck a chord with me that I could not explain . . .

Next day he came back. With a deep yet loving voice he said, 'Hello, Fatimih. How are you today? Any better?' I didn't answer. Then he came closer, bent over my head, lowered his voice and in a lovely tone he asked, 'Is your heart aching with pain?' The resonance of his voice threw me again. I was trying to think who he was. In Iran there had always been a class distinction between educated and uneducated people. In fact, as long as I could remember there had been a marked gap between doctors and patients. A doctor was educated, respected and learned, while the patient was merely there to be treated and nothing more. This doctor, however, seemed to genuinely care about how I was. Unlike other doctors, he had spent time with me and had taken an interest in how I was feeling. Every time he came over and looked at me, I became very shy. I wanted him to talk so I could hear his voice.

On the third day, I smiled at him and said, 'You are a very humble doctor.' He looked pleased and gratified.

Cheerfully he said, 'The operation was successful, wasn't it?' Then he sat at the bottom of my bed and said, 'Fatimih, what is my name?' I searched my soul for his name. Was I supposed to know his name, I asked myself. I felt silly for not having asked one of the nurses beforehand. I desperately wanted to remember this man and prayed that his name would come to me, as more and more he was becoming as familiar to me as I was to myself. Recognizing my struggle, the kind doctor hinted that we had not spoken since we were children.

A wave of emotion that I can never describe came over me. I knew him, just as he knew me. With more joy than I could ever express, I asked him, 'What are you doing here, Nasser?' His whole face lit up. He squeezed my hand harder. There was so much joy in the room. I didn't know where to begin. There was a lifetime to talk about. It was the boy of my childhood, my dearest friend and mentor and the person who had first introduced me to this Faith which had become the purpose for my every living breath. As we began to speak, a nurse walked in and Nasser explained that he had taken a vein from my leg to replace the arteries to my heart. When the nurse left, he joked that this was all he had changed. Nasser said that during the operation he had never stopped praying for my health. He said he had known who I was before the operation, but didn't want to make it harder for me by seeing me then. But he had signed all the necessary forms for the insurance and had made sure I was well looked after.

I could not believe how my life had come full circle. I had never expected to see him again. I told him he was my hero and my saviour. I told him he was the instrument that had attracted me to the Bahá'í Faith and saved me spiritually, and now he was the one who had operated on my heart to save me physically. 'How can I possibly thank you?' I asked him. He said I didn't have to. He said, 'Fatimih, you became a Bahá'í because you were looking for truth and were brave enough to break away from tradition. You had an inquisitive mind and a good heart from childhood.'

Now that the operation was a success, Nasser explained, it would allow him to return to the United States and work there again. I was so happy for him but I wished he did not have to go back. I had just found him. He said that I had helped him without knowing who he was and that meant more than what he had done for me. I was so glad to have been able to be of some assistance, after so many years, to the person who had unknowingly given me so much.

When I asked Nasser why he wanted to go to America, he told me the same story that I had heard so many times before. His family were in America, but because he was a Bahá'í, and in this case because he was so highly skilled, the Government would not allow him to leave the country. His last chance of being reunited with his family was to undertake this experimental procedure and secure a scholarship to further develop the technique in the United States. Not long into our conversation, my family arrived to visit me. I wished I could tell them who he really was but I was too shy to do so then.

From that day on, each day before he went home Nasser came and sat on my bed, held my hand and we talked and talked and talked. He told me he had never forgotten me. He knew I had become a Bahá'í. He had heard the news from his mother but didn't know the rest of my life story. He had gone to America to study and had graduated from a medical school many years ago. Nasser said that everyone in the hospital knew that he was a Bahá'í but that because they needed his expertise they ignored his religion. He said he often thought about the thousands of Bahá'ís who wanted to work but were not permitted to do so. I agreed, and talked about my children, who had been told they were blasphemers, infidels, spies or Zionists and that as a result their services were not required. He whispered in my ear his disappointment and said that the Government had conveniently decided, at least for the time being, that the Bahá'í doctors didn't belong to any group. He said he had made an appointment with the administrative head of the hospital to inform him that he was a Bahá'í. His boss said he couldn't understand why Nasser was pushing the issue when thousands of people were losing their jobs because of their religion. As Nasser rose to leave the man had told him, 'I didn't hear a word of what you said.' From then on, it was understood that Nasser would continue to serve the hospital and his superiors would not consider his religion.

Nasser was now an elderly man, but teaching medicine and discovering new techniques seemed to be his passion. I told him that I had decided to apply for a passport and wanted to go to Australia. I told him about Fere and Faranak and he thought it was a fantastic idea and that I needed a holiday after this massive operation. Then he reminded me of my television interview. His new technique had gained him much publicity, and it had been agreed that the local media would interview me as a condition of him being awarded the scholarship. 'Don't forget to say how great I was,' he said jokingly as he left the room.

The auspicious moment arrived when I had to appear on television. I was tense and a bit sensitive about being questioned regarding my operation and about the person who had saved my life. I was not trusting of these people who converged on me. I was worried about telling the whole nation how wonderful Nasser was, in case they kept him in Iran. At the same time, I knew he would be watching me. It was very difficult to know what the best course of action was. During the interview, I had no problem answering questions regarding the hospital staff, food or other services, but I became emotional when they asked me about the surgeon. With tears in my eyes, I told the interviewer that Iran was very lucky to have such a noble man. I said my heart operation was such a success that I had recovered to the point where I was only taking aspirin, whereas before the operation I had been taking 60 different tablets. I said that if I had the power, I would do anything to support this doctor because he would bring pride to our nation. A week later when I went back for my check-up, I saw Nasser again. He told me he had won his scholarship and was going to the United States.

A month later I came back to Bushehr. A new office had been set up which dealt specifically with passport applications. This office was established essentially to process the large number of applications from people intending to travel to Mecca for pilgrimage. I applied, paid the application fee and was refused on the spot. I believe the message was, 'Don't even bother.' However, I didn't give up. I tried again and was rejected again. Faranak and Fere sent some money for my upkeep. It was hard to resist the temptation. I promised myself that this would be the last time, the last chance. I tried one more time. I was refused, and asked why. I was told that since my marriage was null and void I could not use Mr Saatchi's surname to apply for a passport. I told the official that I had been forced to be married to Mr Saatchi when I was nine years old by a mullah, so the wedding ceremony was registered in the Islamic way. He said there was no record.

Just before the 1979 Revolution, Iranians were required to renew their birth and marriage certificates and to include a photograph of themselves dressed according to the Islamic dress code. I had hoped then that I would be officially registered as Manijeh Saatchi in my new birth certificate. Since there was no record of our marriage and I was using Javad's surname, they would not give me a passport. It was rather confusing. I loved and preferred Javad's name, but I decided to be detached from his name or any name. All I wanted was a passport. I wanted my freedom. I wanted a life with dignity. I wanted a place I could call home.

One day, after hours of prayer and meditation, I went in to the office and handed over a photocopy of my original birth certificate, using my maiden name as I lodged an application for a passport. The official looked at my birth certificate and asked, 'Are you sure this birth certificate is yours?' I said, 'Yes, it is mine.' He said the photo in the birth certificate looked like my grandchild, and I needed to get a new photo for it if he was to renew it. I did that, but still didn't know whether I would be successful. I lived in a place where there was no stability or assurance. The law changed so often and each mullah held a powerful position, to the extent that they could evict you from your house, close down your business, expel you from your school or university. They could order your execution just because you had a different religion. There was so much misunderstanding and inconsistency that it made it very difficult to read between the lines.

So after 40 years of being called Manijeh Saatchi, I reverted to my Muslim name, Fatimih Muhammadi. I had not used it since I became a Bahá'í a few years after my marriage to Javad. I applied for a passport using this name, and fortunately was not interviewed in person. They assumed from my name that I was a Muslim. I applied at a time when a number of women were applying to go to Saudi Arabia, and they thought I was going to Mecca like everybody else. As soon as I received my passport I borrowed money and quickly left for Tehran.

During my interview to get an exit visa, the officer in charge tried to talk me out of leaving Iran, saying, 'Madam, why do you want to go overseas? The Western world is corrupt. You are old, you do not speak the language.' It reminded me of Faranak's interview in Bushehr.

The same old tactic was used. I told him of my daughter's wedding, and when he did not believe me I showed him Faranak's wedding invitation. I insisted that I had to be there to give her my consent. I didn't say anything about giving her away, a term used by many Western countries, because that would sound strange. Iranians don't use that expression. He called the review officer to help him out. I said, 'Sir, my youngest daughter, Faranak, if you may recall, is getting married. Her father has passed away and I wish to be there for her.'

He asked, 'Your name?'

I said, 'Fatimih.'

He asked for my surname and I replied, 'Muhammadi.'

You could not possibly find a more authentic Islamic name for a female in the whole nation. To this day, I am at loss to know whether they recognized me or even knew who Faranak was. All I know is that there was, miraculously, no mention of the Bahá'í Faith. They didn't ask for any additional information and I didn't volunteer any. Having obtained an exit visa, I applied for an entry visa from the Australian Embassy. My application was approved and within days I got the visa. Fere promptly booked and paid for a return ticket, arranged for it to be picked up at the airport, and sent a letter with contact names, telephone numbers and addresses. She also put in some Australian dollars in case I needed to call her on the way. There was also a card inside the envelope. On one side it said, in Persian, 'Mum, carry this card with your travel documents all the time,' and on the other side it said in English:

> My name is Fatimih Muhammadi. I do not speak English. After 23 years I am going to be reunited with my daughter. I am going to Sydney in Australia through Kuala Lumpur in Malaysia. Please help me get there. My daughter's telephone number is (061) 2965 7123.

This card gave me the confidence I needed. I felt strong and capable of travelling on my own. The thought of my age never crossed my mind, and I guess I didn't even contemplate my health. I was so excited about the whole thing that I'd forgotten my heart surgery. There was nothing that could stop me now. As I was leaving the country, I wished I could have taken my grandchildren with me. They all said, 'See you soon.'

Once at the airport, I felt very frightened that someone, out of jealousy, might have leaked the information to officials that I had got my passport under false pretences. I was so agitated and distressed about not declaring I was a Bahá'í that if I had a choice between death and being found out, I would have chosen death. I felt worse when my name was called out on the loudspeaker. I remembered Fere. What if they said my passport was not classified? What if they asked me to go to room number 13? I must admit that it was very difficult for me to be positive. I had prayed and meditated a lot before I left the house that day, but the worry seemed to be staying with me. I think prayer gives one the coping mechanism, but it does not necessarily solve one's problems the way one wants them to be solved. Right now, I wanted my mind and heart to be at peace.

When I reached the service counter I was given my passport. The officer showed me the red stamp and explained that it indicated a once-only use, but that I could extend the visa if I needed to stay longer. I had heard this before. Tourists are given a red visa as opposed to a green exit visa. By now I was very excited, because I felt sure that someone was taking care of me. I recalled Fere's experience of trying to leave legally and Faranak's dangerous journey across the border illegally. I said, 'Thank you, Lord, for understanding my limits.' It seemed to me that at that moment I could not handle any more tests and my God knew that. This experience confirmed my belief that we are here to learn, develop and flourish. We are not on this planet to suffer for no reason. Fortunately, everything went ahead smoothly. I sat down in the plane, closed my eyes and forgot all about my problems. I remembered 'Abdu'l-Bahá's saying, 'Joy gives us wings! In times of joy our strength is more vital, our intellect keener, and our understanding less clouded. We seem better able to cope with the world and to find our sphere of influence.' I said farewell to my homeland. I joyfully cried for my country. I cried for my children. I cried for my beloved husband buried in an unknown place. As I looked through the window, the sky was so vast that it seemed to have swallowed up the plane. Eventually, we reached Malaysia and everyone was happy to have left the first part of the journey behind.

A couple of young women on the trip asked me to remove my Islamic head cover, saying that it would be better if we appeared to be modern women rather than being covered. I went to our hotel, had a shower and got changed but I could not take off the head cover. I saw the women downstairs and they took off my *chador*. However, I insisted on wearing the scarf. I realized then that the tradition had done its damage. Wearing a *chador* had become so much a part of me that it was going to take a while to get used to not wearing it. When we went shopping that night I was very self-conscious. We had dinner together and celebrated our freedom.

The next day we flew to Sydney. As usual, I prayed for the safety of all the passengers. A hostess stood in the middle of the aisle for the safety instructions, and her gestures were so clear and meaningful that without understanding a word of what she was saying I felt I knew what I was supposed to be doing if anything went wrong. She had lovely facial expressions and looked much friendlier than the other hostesses I had met so far. I was just about to fall asleep when a gentle voice that seemed to come from a delicate face stroked my ear. I turned towards the voice and saw the arms of the same hostess stretched towards me holding a tray of food. I smiled and said, 'Merci,' thank you. She seemed to understand. I touched my heart and said, 'My heart is so big you can fit the world in it.' She smiled again.

As time went on, it became increasingly difficult for me to concentrate. The big moment was approaching. My thoughts turned dreamily to Fere and Faranak, my grandchildren and my son-in-law. When I heard the voice of the hostess on the microphone, I knew we were close. I eagerly looked through the window at the city of

Sydney. The plane landed at 4 a.m., it was a lovely fresh morning and the airport was busy with activity.

By six o'clock all the passengers had gone but I was still standing in the airport and thought that perhaps I had landed in the wrong city. I tried to ask someone, but they didn't understand. I became emotional. I was very tired and went to sit down. An airport officer noticed me and said something. All of a sudden I burst into tears. She sat down next to me and was so nice I thought she was going to take my pulse, but she said something and, without any hesitation, reached out for my tickets and papers. I felt that I could trust her and that she was going to look into it.

I was right. With the help of an interpreter, she contacted Fere by telephone. She was talking to Fere when I noticed my son-in-law, Abbas, coming from a distance. I had not seen him for nearly 15 years. He had less hair, but his smile, his nice set of white teeth and his shiny glasses looked reassuringly familiar. I was delighted to see him and gave him a hearty hug and kisses. He apologized for being late, blaming his own flight for the delay. He helped me carry my luggage from the international airport to the domestic terminal. I felt privileged to have him as a son-in-law in our family. Enveloped with the brightness of that autumn day, I thanked God for living and loving and experiencing such a wonderful golden day.

As we were getting closer to the domestic airport, he gently and quietly asked me if I would mind putting my scarf away. He said we were in Sydney and there was no need for an Islamic veil. I laughed. He laughed too. 'You find it amusing, do you?' he asked.

I said, 'Just tell me how many more planes I need to catch before we reach home?'

He did not get it. He asked 'Why?'

I said, 'I'm afraid I don't have many clothes on.'

Abbas laughed. I explained to him what had happened when we were in Kuala Lumpur, and that if I kept removing an item of clothing at every airport I would soon have nothing on. He reassured me that that flight was the last flight before we reached home.

In Canberra, all the members of the family received me. It was a warm welcome and a beautiful way to begin a new life.

A year after her wedding, Faranak had a baby girl. Fere and I began working hard on rebuilding the relationship we had never had as mother and daughter. Twenty-three years is a long time not to have your child. We were getting to know each other all over again.

One day, when we were strolling down the footpath, Fere asked me to tell her what she could do to please me. My immediate response was, 'What can I do to compensate for the 23 years I was denied the opportunity to help my child?' Fere convinced me that every mother does her best and that I too had done my best, given the circumstances we had been in. She said that I would not have been able to do anything for her even if we had been free to be together, because she had left home when she was 18 and got married, and left the country of her own volition when she was 19. On the other hand, Fere said that she had never appreciated what Javad and I had done for her. This wisdom, she believed, had come through experience of being a mother herself, not reading about it. So she wanted to do something for me to make up for the years she should have looked after me.

I told Fere that I had always wanted to write a book about the history of the House of Báb in Bushehr, but given that we were in Australia and I could not write in English, how about if she wrote the book? Fere hugged me with joy and thought writing the book was a brilliant idea. She agreed to do it if I would tell her the story.

That was how I ended up staying in Australia forever. Fere applied to keep me safe in Australia, and on 10 June 1998 I was granted a permanent visa. I became the happiest person anyone could imagine. Fere and Faranak were very pleased and we all celebrated the good news together.

Epilogue

by Fere Hooshmand

This book reveals a story of the heroic life of a Bahá'í in Iran. It is historic because it is the first time that the story of the House of the Báb in Bushehr has been told. It is also my mother's story, because she was the custodian of that holy place.

My enthusiasm for our joint project was so great that I thought I might finish writing the book before she finished telling the story! Following the decision of the Australian Immigration Department to grant my mother a permanent visa, I wrote a submission to the Arts Council of Australia under the Multicultural Grant Scheme to ask for financial help for our book, and received a letter congratulating me on winning a small grant. That was how the telling of Manijeh's story began.

To understand this story is to understand many things about the Bahá'í Faith. My mother was born into a strict Shi'ite Muslim family, yet her independence of thought and spirit led her to embrace a new religion, one which for her encapsulated all that was good in Islam and added so much more.

Iran (Persia) stands at the crossroads of world civilizations. To the north is the Caspian Sea, the largest lake in the world. If you journey to the south, you cross a vast desert where nomads live. Iran prides itself on its long and illustrious history, but it has also had dark periods of oppression and desolation. It is a country that has squandered much of its heritage. It has a rich traditional literature. Omar Khayyam wrote his Rubaiyyat in the 12th century, 100 years before Hafiz and Sa'di of Shiraz (known as the Court Poets) began writing. Sa'di became famous after he wrote two books – the *Gulistan* (Rose Garden) and the *Bustan* (Fruit Garden). Other great poets such as Rumi also came from Persia.

This book introduces a new idea, a new vision that has emerged out of the old Persia through the teachings of Bahá'u'lláh, the Founder of the Bahá'í Faith. This vision led my mother not only to change her name but her whole way of life. She believes that this vision and these teachings, given the opportunity, have the potential to inspire all human beings to care deeply for mankind and the natural environment. Fundamental to the vision for the future of humanity is the view that nothing is an entire body of itself; each brick is a piece of the temple, an element of the whole. Each nation plays an essential part and are all part of one human family.

This vision of the oneness of mankind changed my mother's life spiritually, although she suffered persecution and was ostracized in her own country. For her the question remains: how can the body have peace when pieces are missing? We hope that through this heroic life story you may glimpse a part of this vision, that will empower you, your family and your community to make the world a better place.

If you have enjoyed this book,
why not read more personal stories?

WHEN REASON SLEEPS

by Audrey Mellard

Manuchihr was waiting for a bus to take him from Qazvin, Iran, to his home in Tehran when a taxi with several men in it pulled up alongside him. He waved it away but was told to get in, they would make room for him. Since they were all heavily armed, he realized that he had no option but to obey. The driver pulled away sharply from the bus stop.

Manuchihr protested but was told, 'You have some questions to answer.'

He was driven to a building which he remembered as having once belonged to friends of his. Now it was the court of the Revolutionary Guard. It was 1 May 1982.

Mehrangiz 'Mehri' Farzaneh-Moayyad relates the story of her husband, who was arbitrarily arrested, imprisoned and executed in Iran, and recounts her own imprisonment in a squalid prison a year after her husband's execution, and her dramatic escape across the Iranian desert on camelback with her young daughter to refuge in Pakistan and, at last, to her new home in Scotland.

When Reason Sleeps is Mehri's story as told to Audrey Mellard, who has gathered the threads into a compelling narrative of the hope, spiritual strength, courage and faith of a family whose only crime was that they were Bahá'ís.

KNIGHT WITH A BRIEFCASE

The Life of Knight of Bahá'u'lláh Ezzat Zahrai

by Judith Kaye Logsdon-Dubois

Writer Judith Kaye Logsdon-Dubois thought that a businessman's only goal in life was to make as much money as possible and that he could have nothing to say that would interest her – that is, until she met Ezzat Zahrai.

One day she found herself sitting on a terrace of a house in southwest France listening to the former division president of a multinational company speak of spirituality, of visions, of ideals, of mystic experiences, of hardships, prison and persecution, of truth, of destiny, of God. In his youth he had set out alone from Iran for Africa to bring the teachings of the Bahá'í Faith to what is now Zimbabwe for the very first time.

As he told his story, Ms Logsdon-Dubois found Mr Zahrai cared very little about the status of wealth, that he had no taste for luxury. She felt he would have unhesitatingly sacrificed his life for the Faith he believed in. Through his adventures in a new land he had become a modern-day knight, a knight with a briefcase.

Judith Kaye Logsdon-Dubois has captured the essence of Ezzat Zahrai – his humour and good nature, his business ethics, his strong belief in the oneness of humanity and his passion for telling others about the Bahá'í Faith.

NEGOTIATING SHADOWS

by Grace Growing Medicine E. R.

Alcohol/drug addiction is a worldwide problem. But it is also a personal problem. Grace Growing Medicine E.R. knows: it was her problem.

Negotiating Shadows traces her life from her birth into poverty and an abusive childhood into her womanhood as an addict. We accompany her on her dark journey as she negotiates the conflicts of life towards a spiritual awakening. On her way to the Sun she found Alcoholics Anonymous and the Bahá'í Faith. This is all set against the historical and social highlights of the period.

AGAINST INCREDIBLE ODDS

Life of a 20th Century Iranian Bahá'í Family

by Baharieh Rouhani Ma'ani

Against Incredible Odds: Life of a 20th Century Iranian Bahá'í Family tells the story of a family from the Iranian town of Nayríz whose life has spanned the whole history of the Bahá'í Faith, from its earliest days to the present. Their story is the story of the Bahá'í Cause itself.

The Rouhani family was a direct witness to the growth of the Bahá'í Faith and also to its persecution, from the time of Bahá'u'lláh, through the ministries of 'Abdu'l-Bahá and Shoghi Effendi and to the establishment and flowering of the Universal House of Justice. At every turn the family faced major misfortunes – fires, floods, the untimely death of their children and spouses, as well as the persecution and difficulties that swept over the Bahá'í community – yet at every turn they served the Faith as its defenders, teachers and pioneers.

It is a story of lifelong struggle against incredible odds, of renouncing worldly pleasures to achieve higher aims, of accepting material deprivations to gain spiritual strength and of forgoing the desire of wanting to be physically close to one's children – the cherished desire of every parent – to enable them to scatter far and wide and work towards the achievement of Bahá'u'lláh's pivotal goal of unifying humankind.

LEGACY OF COURAGE

The Life of Ola Pawlowska, Knight of Bahá'u'lláh

by Suzanne Schuurman

Here is the story of a remarkable life that began in the Austro-Hungarian Empire of Franz Joseph, spanned two World Wars, and played out on three continents.

Born into the Polish aristocracy, Ola Pawlowska was told she would never have to earn her living. War and early widowhood changed all that. Fleeing Nazi-occupied France to Canada with her young daughter, Ola worked at various jobs, mainly as a secretary at the Polish Legation – but in Canada she also encountered the Bahá'í Faith, and in 1953 she became a Knight of Bahá'u'lláh to the St Pierre and Miquelon Islands off the Canadian coast.

But the services for which she is best remembered still lay ahead. Pioneering to the Congo in the early 1960s fulfilled a life-long dream to live in Africa. She was to stay for the next thirty years, loved by many and courageously confronting the many challenges of a rapidly expanding Bahá'í community in a country with vast distances to be covered.

And in her eighties, Ola Pawlowska pioneered yet again – to her beloved homeland of Poland, where she saw the establishment of Poland's first National Spiritual Assembly.

Beautifully written by Ola's daughter, Suzanne Schuurman, Ola's story will be an inspiration to all those who possess the spirit of adventure.

O MY BROTHER!

The Story of a Search after Truth

by Madeline Hellaby

One morning in war-time Britain a schoolteacher gives a little yellow pamphlet to a fellow bus passenger. And so William Hellaby, a life-long seeker after truth, is launched on his first investigation of the Bahá'í Faith, but in the end he decides instead to train for the ministry in the Unitarian church. After a ten-year interval, and now recently married to a woman whose family's Unitarian church membership goes back 200 years, Billie embarks with his wife on his second examination of the Bahá'í Faith. Their studies throw new light on Gospel teachings, challenge long-held ideas and beliefs, and bring them closer to Christ than ever before. Growing commitment to the teachings of Bahá'u'lláh faces them with moral decisions and the fact that acceptance of the Bahá'í Faith will bring loss of home and livelihood for a family with three young children, and plunges them into crisis. Eventually, even Grandpa becomes interested . . .

This thoughtful and challenging account, in which Madeline Hellaby relates how she and her husband investigated the Bahá'í Faith, will appeal particularly to readers wishing to understand something of the questions facing students of the Faith from Christian denominations.

www.ingramcontent.com/pod-product-compliance
Ingram Content Group UK Ltd.
Pitfield, Milton Keynes, MK11 3LW, UK
UKHW040007200726
13854UKWH00001B/82

9 780853 985723